DIVERSE HISTORIES

BLOOMSBURY EDUCATION

Bloomsbury Publishing Plc

50 Bedford Square, London, WC1B 3DP, UK

29 Earlsfort Terrace, Dublin 2, Ireland

BLOOMSBURY, BLOOMSBURY EDUCATION and the Diana logo are trademarks of Bloomsbury Publishing Plc

First published in Great Britain, 2022 by Bloomsbury Publishing Plc

Text copyright © The National Archives, 2022

Images Crown Copyright © Reproduced with permission of The National Archives, 2022 (unless otherwise stated)

The National Archives logo © Crown Copyright, 2022

Clare Horrie and Rachel Hillman have asserted their rights under the Copyright,
Designs and Patents Act, 1988, to be identified as Authors of this work

Every reasonable effort has been made to trace copyright holders of material reproduced in this book,
but if any have been inadvertently overlooked the publishers would be glad to hear from them

Bloomsbury Publishing Plc does not have any control over, or responsibility for, any third-party websites
referred to or in this book. All internet addresses given in this book were correct at the time of going to press.
The authors and publisher regret any inconvenience caused if addresses have changed or sites have ceased to exist,
but can accept no responsibility for any such changes

All rights reserved. This book may be photocopied, for use in the educational establishment for which it was
purchased, but may not be reproduced in any other form or by any other means – graphic, electronic,
or mechanical, including photocopying, recording, taping or information storage or retrieval systems
– without prior permission in writing of the publishers

A catalogue record for this book is available from the British Library

ISBN: PB: 978-1-8019-9050-9; ePDF: 978-1-8019-9052-3; ePub: 978-1-8019-9053-0

2 4 6 8 10 9 7 5 3 1 (paperback)

Interior design and typesetting by Janene Spencer

Printed and bound in the UK by CPI Group Ltd, CR0 4YY

MIX
Paper from responsible sources
FSC® C013604

To find out more about our authors and books visit www.bloomsbury.com and sign up for our newsletters

DIVERSE HISTORIES

A source book for teaching Black, Asian and minority ethnic histories at Key Stage 3

CLARE HORRIE and RACHEL HILLMAN
with contributions from ELA KACZMARSKA

BLOOMSBURY EDUCATION

LONDON OXFORD NEW YORK NEW DELHI SYDNEY

CONTENTS

Introduction — 8

Foreword — 11

Part 1: The development of Church, state and society in medieval Britain 1066–1509 and in Britain 1509–1745 — 13

	Lesson	Topic	Date	Page
1	A Black figure in the Domesday Abbreviato	Society in medieval England	1086	14
2	John Blanke	Society in Tudor England	1507	17
3	Black Tudors	Society in Elizabethan England	1596	21
4	Jean Barbot	Society in seventeenth-century West Africa	1682	25

Part 2: Ideas, political power, industry and empire: Britain, 1745–1901 — 29

	Lesson	Topic	Date	Page
5	Seventeenth-century Jamaica	Jamaica and the British Empire	1698	30
6	Black Georgians	Society in Georgian Britain	1746	33
7	The 'Black Poor'	Society in Georgian Britain	1780s	36
8	Slavery in Bermuda	Slavery	1786	39
9	Resistance to slavery in St Vincent	Slavery	1786	43
10	Olaudah Equiano	Slavery	1792	46
11	William Davidson	Cato Street Conspiracy	1820	49
12	The Jamaican Slave Rebellion	Slavery	1832	53
13	William Cuffey	Chartist Movement	1834	56
14	Mary Seacole	Crimean War	1869	60
15	The Jubilee Singers	Musical culture in Victorian Britain	1870s	63
16	Samuel Coleridge-Taylor	Musical culture in Victorian Britain	1875–1901	68
17	Adbul Karim	Queen Victoria's household	1894	71
18	The British Empire in the Victorian period	British Empire	1895	74

CONTENTS

Part 3: Challenges for Britain, Europe and the wider world: 1901 to the present day 77

	Lesson	Topic	Date	Page
19	Sophia Duleep Singh	Suffragettes	1912	78
20	Walter Tull	First World War	1914	81
21	Naik Darwan Sing Negi	First World War	1914–1918	84
22	Jemadar Mir Dast	First World War	1915	87
23	Euan Lucie-Smith	First World War	1915	90
24	Chinese Labour Corps in the First World War	First World War	1917	94
25	Indian Labour Corps in the First World War	First World War	1919	97
26	The 1919 Race Riots	Race relations in post-war Britain	1919	100
27	Massacre in Amritsar	Life in post-war India	1920	103
28	The British Empire in the 1920s	British Empire	1920s	106
29	Shapurji Saklatvala MP	1920s politics	1922	109
30	Marcus Garvey in Britain	Civil rights movement	1928	112
31	The League of Coloured Peoples	Civil rights movement	1935	115
32	Indian airmen in the Second World War	Second World War	1939	118
33	Caribbean airmen in the Second World War	Second World War	1939	121
34	African soldiers in the Second World War	Second World War	1939	124
35	Gold Coast in the Second World War	Second World War	1939–1945	127
36	Nursing in the Second World War	Second World War	1939–1945	130
37	Industry in India in the Second World War	Second World War	1939	133
38	West Indies Calling	Second World War	1944	136
39	Noor Inayat Khan	Second World War	1945	139
40	Racial discrimination in the Second World War	Second World War	1945	143
41	Indian soldiers in the Second World War	Second World War	1947	146
42	The Partition of India	Partition of India	1947	149
43	The Empire Windrush	The Windrush Generation	1948	152
44	Sam Beaver King	The Windrush Generation	1948	155

	Lesson	Topic	Date	Page
45	The Causeway Green 'Riots'	The Windrush Generation	1949	158
46	'A West Indian in England'	The Windrush Generation	1949	161
47	The Independence of Ghana	Independence of African nations	1957	164
48	Paul Robeson	Political protest in 1950s Britain	1959	167
49	Louis Martin	Race relations in 1960s Britain	1966	170
50	Immigrant experiences in 1960s Britain	Race relations in 1960s Britain	1960s	173
51	The Independence of Tanganyika	Independence of African nations	1961	176
52	The Independence of Trinidad and Tobago	Independence of Caribbean nations	1962	179
53	The Independence of Barbados	Independence of Caribbean nations	1967	182
54	Sislin Fay Allen	Multiculturalism in 1960s Britain	1968	185
55	The Race Relations Act 1968	Race relations in 1960s Britain	1968	188
56	Notting Hill Carnival	Race relations in 1960s Britain	1970s	191
57	The British Black Panthers	Black Power in 1970s Britain	1970s	194
58	The Mangrove Nine	Police relations with the Black community	1971	197
59	SUS Law	Police relations with the Black community	1970s and 1980s	200
60	The Brixton riots	Police relations with the Black community	1981	203

INTRODUCTION

This book contains 60 lessons to help transform your students' learning experience in Key Stage 3 history by helping you to integrate more diverse histories into your schemes of work. The vast majority of lessons are based on original sources from our very own government National Archives collections. We hope to build on the concept that archival sources can be used as evidence to investigate and understand the past.

Diverse Histories is not intended as a 'text book' or 'topic book', but as a resource to provide starter lessons to enrich and diversify the topics that you may already teach. It is not our purpose to provide a detailed historical explanation of a particular topic, however, we do provide the historical context for the sources we have included to show the fit within the curriculum.

It is important to note that some of the sources which appear in this book cover sensitive historical subjects. Some reflect language and concepts that are entirely unacceptable and inappropriate today and this has been highlighted in the captions with the source. We suggest that teachers look at the material carefully before introducing it to their students. It would be helpful to discuss with them the use of language and ideas contained in such material beforehand. Teachers may wish to break down the sources into smaller extracts if they find the sources too long or difficult in any way.

All lessons are rooted in an enquiry-led approach and based on a single archival source. Each lesson includes teacher's notes which explore the following questions: What is this source?, What can we infer from this source?, Why does The National Archives have this source? and What is the context of this source? We also provide an enquiry question, suggested activity and ideas for taking learning further. The enquiry activity varies, for example, it may involve employing the concept of 'the mystery document', or the 'five-second rule'. Prompt questions are also given as a guide for each source, which are generally used creatively as part of the lesson enquiry. Of course there are also certain universal questions that should be applied to all sources when students start to investigate them, some of which are listed at the end of this introduction. We hope that working with sources in this way will help students to frame their own historically valid questions and help them to create written narratives and analyses.

The 'Exploring further' section within the lesson plan is designed to grow subject knowledge and research skills. Here, we have suggested particular tasks and activities. Often, we have also recommended particular texts for teachers on the topic, with suggestions for how they might be used.

The following types of sources form the basis of the lessons in this book: photographs, government reports, telegrams, cartoons, posters, police reports, minutes, manuscripts, maps, private and official letters, film production notes and newspapers. We hope that encountering such a rich range of source types will expose pupils to the stuff of history while strengthening their skills in handling primary evidence and helping them to form their own interpretations.

The 60 lessons in this book will support teachers in delivering the key aims of the

'Crowds campaign for Independence, March 1961' (CO 1069/166 (12)). Photograph of a demonstration in favour of independence for Tanganyika.

National Curriculum in history to support understanding of 'the diversity of societies and relationships between different groups, as well as their own identity and the challenges of their time' and to ensure that all students understand the methods of historical enquiry.

All of the lessons reflect the Key Stage 3 history National Curriculum content offering. Therefore, teachers looking for sources relating to such themes as the development of Church, state and society in medieval Britain 1066–1509; the development of Church, state and society in Britain 1509–1745; ideas, political power, industry and empire: Britain 1745–1901; and challenges for Britain, Europe and the wider world 1901 to the present day, will find help in this book. The lessons are all based on The National Archives' collections and are not readily found in existing textbooks. They offer a unique way for secondary school students to access real historical documents rather than having to work with secondary texts and narrative histories. For example, you will find lesson enquiries on medieval trumpeter John Blanke, Second World War spy Noor Inayat Khan, Cato Street conspirator William Davidson, singer and civil rights campaigner Paul Robeson, composer Samuel Coleridge-Taylor and the Victorian Jubilee Singers. There are also diverse stories for BAME men and women, about the famous and not so famous, reflecting stories of agency and resistance.

INTRODUCTION

We hope that teachers will be encouraged by this book to make use of their local archives and The National Archives as historians, and to use it to signpost the type of records that can be used to research further diverse histories.

Finally, our lessons could also be used appropriately to support both English and PSHE curriculums at Key Stage 3.

General questions for sources

Identification

- What type of document is it?
- Who produced it? Do you know anything about the author/creator?
- When was it written/produced?
- Why was it written/produced?

Understanding

- Consider the key words and their meaning within the source.
- What points or arguments are made in the source?
- What values or attitudes does the content of the source reflect?
- How does the content of the source relate to a given historical situation?
- Are there any clues about the intended audience for the source?
- How reliable is the source and does it have any limitations?
- How does the source relate to other sources from this period? Does it share the same ideas, attitudes and arguments? How would you explain any differences between sources? (For when looking at several sources on the same topic.)

Clare Horrie and Rachel Hillman

FOREWORD

Being asked to write a foreword for a Key Stage 3 resource book about a subject that I dropped at the first opportunity at school is certainly something I'd never anticipated. Yet my story isn't unusual, with research from the History Matters group showing that history is the third least popular subject at university amongst students of African and Caribbean heritage, despite great interest at community level.[1]

By exploring records at The National Archives and asking critical questions about why government departments including the Home Office, the Colonial Office, the Foreign and Commonwealth Office, and so forth, collected them, this important resource aims to inspire a more inclusive approach to teaching history, and to challenge the sense of alienation felt in many classrooms.

As the official archive of the UK Government (and as what some have described as 'The Babylon Archive'), The National Archives does more often than not represent the voice of officialdom, and many of the records that relate to Black, Asian and minority ethnic communities have unfortunately been gained from the over-policing and surveillance of them. However, and as this text deftly shows, there are also countless examples of community voices represented as well – be it in letters of protest made to the Commission for Racial Equality and other bodies, or in the campaign material of activist groups apprehended by the police – the archives are a rich resource of records of resistance and struggles for social justice and change, waiting to inspire the next generation of historians.

This work marks a timely and significant contribution to the teaching of Key Stage 3 history, and will be an invaluable resource in Britain's multicultural classrooms. Had it been available thirty years earlier, my relationship with history at school might have been very different.

Kevin Searle

---

[1] Adi, H. (2019) *Black British History: New Perspectives.* London: Zed, p. 2.

PART 1

THE DEVELOPMENT OF CHURCH, STATE AND SOCIETY IN MEDIEVAL BRITAIN 1066–1509 AND IN BRITAIN 1509–1745

LESSON 1

A BLACK FIGURE IN THE DOMESDAY ABBREVIATO

CONNECTION TO THE CURRICULUM

The development of Church, state and society in medieval Britain 1066–1509

Aim: To find out about the different types of people living in England at the time of the Domesday Abbreviato.

Historical figure: Black figure in the Abbreviato

Source: Black figure on illuminated initial from Abbreviato of The Domesday Book (E36/284 f.196)

TEACHER'S NOTES

What is this source?

This image comes from the Domesday Abbreviato, a working document used by officials of the King's Exchequer to consult the original volumes of the Domesday Book. It is one of three abbreviated versions of the Domesday Book that was produced in the thirteenth century.

What can we infer from this source?

The Abbreviato is written in Latin and each page has been intricately illustrated. This page is decorated with the image of a Black man holding onto the letter 'I' and is the opening letter to an entry about the King's land in Derbyshire. This illustration tells us that at this early time, there were already Black people living in England. Perhaps the scribe had seen a person of African descent who had come across to England following one of the Crusades.

The Black man is dressed in a short tunic over hose, which suggests that he is a man of lower status, maybe a labourer or a peasant. Those of higher status, such as kings, are illustrated with long, flowing robes within the Abbreviato.

Why does The National Archives have this source?

This source comes from the Abbreviato in the records of the Exchequer and was a working document for officials. They used the Domesday Book to calculate and collect tax for the Crown, and the Abbreviato was a working document that they added information to as they worked.

What is the context of this source?

The Domesday Book was commissioned in 1085–1086 by King William I, who wanted to find out how much his new kingdom was worth and therefore how much tax he could command from his subjects. It was written in Latin, the official language of the Church and government records at the time.

Domesday is a significant document for helping historians to find out about aspects of life in medieval England. For example, we can find out about the different types of people who lived there and the way in which society was organised (although Domesday does contain very little information on women, and no information on children!).

Domesday reveals how the land was divided and used, with lots of woodland, meadows and pastures. Much of the land was used for farming, although some people did live in small towns and worked in different trades. It also shows us who 'held' the land and how much control King William, his tenants-in-chief and the Church had.

The Domesday Book is not as old as the Black presence in Britain. Africans first arrived with the Roman Empire when Britain was invaded in the year 43 AD.

Diverse Histories © Clare Horrie and Rachel Hillman, 2022

LESSON IDEAS

ENQUIRY QUESTION
What does this document reveal about society in Britain at the time of the Abbreviato?

Getting started

You can use this document to further develop students' understanding about the information that the Domesday Book contains and what it can reveal about society in medieval Britain.

Start by showing the students the source and asking them to describe what they can see. Accept some general observations about the source. Students will most likely point out that it's an extract from a handwritten document showing an illustration of a man. Depending on their prior knowledge, some students may be able to date the source roughly to medieval times.

Now share some further information about the source. Tell the students that it is an extract from the Domesday Abbreviato. Using the teacher's notes above, explain what the Abbreviato is and how it was used.

Next, focus in on the figure of the man, noting that it is a depiction of a Black man and inviting further observations. If you need to prompt the students, you can use the following suggested questions:

- Who do you think the man is?
- How is he dressed?
- Is he important? Why/why not?

Finish the enquiry activity with a class discussion about why the scribe might have illustrated a Black man on this page. What does this reveal about society at this time?

Exploring further

Discuss with students the fact that Black people have been present in Britain for at least two millennia. Some Black people would have come to Britain when the Romans invaded in 43 AD and they formed an integral part of British society throughout the medieval ages and beyond. Evidence can be found showing they enlisted in the armed forces, married in parish churches, engaged with literary and artistic life, worked as servants in country houses and challenged the repressive laws of the day.

Share with the students further stories, documents and evidence relating to Black presence in medieval Britain. There are a number to choose from on this BBC Bitesize article, such as Bartholomew, who was a 'man on the run' in Nottingham, and the 'Ipswich Man', who was buried in a monastery in Ipswich: **www.bbc.co.uk/bitesize/articles/z8gpm39**

Follow-up tasks

- Use the internet to find out more about one of the stories explored in the BBC article. Write a report that details the information that is available and highlights any key information that is missing.

16 Diverse Histories © Clare Horrie and Rachel Hillman, 2022

LESSON 2

JOHN BLANKE

> **CONNECTION TO THE CURRICULUM**
> The development of Church, state and society in Britain 1509–1745
> **Aim:** To find out about the presence of Black people in Tudor times.
> **Historical figure:** John Blanke (fl. 1501–1511)
> **Source:** John Blanke's wage-slip, December 1507 (E36/214 f.109)

TEACHER'S NOTES

What is this source?

This document is a wage-slip for a man called John Blanke, taken from the records of the Treasurer of the Chamber (the person who looked after the royal finances). It is dated 1507.

What can we infer from this source?

This wage-slip is handwritten and the style of writing can help us to date the document. It's written in English and makes reference to a man called John Blanke, 'the blacke Trumpet'; this means that John Blanke was a trumpeter and the provenance of the record tells us that he played in the royal court. He must have been an accomplished musician to play to such an important audience! 'Blacke' is being used to describe the colour of his skin, and we can tell from the document that he is being paid his wages for the month of November. He was paid 20 shillings, which in today's money would be around £430. To be paid such a sum suggests that John Blanke had worked every day of the month.

Why does The National Archives have this source?

This record comes from an Exchequer roll and is part of information relating to the royal finances, kept by the Treasurer of the Chamber.

What is the context of this source?

John Blanke, the black trumpeter, played at the courts of both Henry VII and then Henry VIII. There are a number of payments made to John Blanke in the records of the Treasurer of the Chamber, spanning across the two kings' reigns. He was paid 8 shillings a day, a sum that was kept the same by both kings.

John Blanke performed at momentous occasions such as the funeral of Henry VII and the coronation of Henry VIII. Amongst The National Archives' records there is also a petition from Blanke regarding his demand for a wage increase, reflecting that he was not afraid to stand up for his rights and to make his case known. He wanted to be paid the same amount as other trumpeters at the time.

Some historians have argued that Blanke was not John's real surname, but one given to him as a derisive reference to the colour of his skin. 'Blanc' is the French word for 'white'. However, there is no firm evidence for this.

John Blanke was not the only Black man living in Tudor England. For example, Catherine of Aragon, Henry VIII's first wife, had brought many servants across to England from Spain in 1501, including Africans. Countries such as Spain and Portugal would have had more contact with Africa at this time through trade, and from there, Black people would have then made their passage across to Britain.

💡 LESSON IDEAS

ENQUIRY QUESTION

What does this document reveal about the presence of Black people in Tudor England?

Getting started

Use this document to introduce students to the fact that there were hundreds of Black people living in England at this time.

Show students the document and ask them to examine the source in pairs or groups. Before providing the transcript, or any further information about the source, ask the students to see if they can decipher any of the Tudor handwriting. Can they make out any of the words? What do they think the document is about at this stage?

Invite pairs or groups to share their initial thoughts with the rest of the class. Accept all answers and observations, and then hand out the transcript. What do the students understand about the document now?

Once you've heard the students' thoughts, confirm some basic information regarding the source, namely that it is the wage-slip of John Blanke, a trumpeter in Tudor England who played in the royal court and who was a Black man.

Once the students have had time to look through the transcript again and have a good understanding about the provenance of the document and what it tells us, ask them to consider the following in their pairs or groups:

- What does the presence of Blanke in a royal court tell us about his standing and ability as a musician at the time?
- Why do you think that reference has been made to the colour of Blanke's skin?
- What other sources could help us to find out more about Blanke and also about the Black presence in Tudor England?

Exploring further

Show students images of the Westminster Tournament Roll. Explain why Henry VIII had it commissioned, and how John Blanke appears on this pictorial record. The Westminster Tournament was held in 1511 to celebrate the birth of Henry VIII and Catherine of Aragon's son (who went on to die in infancy). The Roll was a pictorial record of the Tournament and shows John Blanke on horseback, playing his trumpet as part of the pageant. You can find out more and access the image at the following link:

www.nationalarchives.gov.uk/pathways/blackhistory/early_times/blanke.htm

Pose the following question to students. They can answer this question by writing a short essay or discuss it in a group or as a class:

- What can the Westminster Tournament Roll reveal about Blanke and why he has been included in this magnificent pageant?

Follow-up tasks

- Introduce students to the historian Miranda Kaufmann and her book *Black Tudors*. You can find a video of Kaufmann explaining why she wrote the book here and show this to the students: **www.mirandakaufmann.com/black-tudors.html**
- What else can this reveal about the Black presence in Tudor England?

Diverse Histories © Clare Horrie and Rachel Hillman, 2022

LESSON 2
John Blanke

TRANSCRIPT

Item to John blanke the blacke Trumpet for his moneth wages of Novembre last passed at viij d the day –	xx s. [20 *shillings*]
Item to Sir Rice ap Thomas' servant that brought metheglee to the king for his reward xx s [20 *shillings*] and for the cariage of the same xx s [20 *shillings*]	xl s. [40 *shillings*]
Summa parles	lx s. [60 *shillings*]
S[u]m totals of this wek aforesaid	Lix li iiijs vijd [£59, 4 *shillings*, 7 *pence*]

LESSON 3

BLACK TUDORS

CONNECTION TO THE CURRICULUM
The development of Church, state and society in Britain 1509–1745
Aim: To investigate Black presence in Elizabethan England.
Historical figure: Elizabeth I
Source: Letter from Elizabeth I to the mayors and sheriffs of the country (PC 2/21 f.304)
Caution: This source contains language that is inappropriate and unacceptable today.

TEACHER'S NOTES

What is this source?

This letter, from Elizabeth I addressed to the mayors and sheriffs of the country, dated 11th July 1596, concerned actions to be taken against 'Blackmoores' in England. It is a Privy Council record. This series includes documents which minutes its proceedings, its orders, certain proclamations and the papers accompanying them.

What can we infer from this source?

The term 'Blackamoor' at this time was used to refer to any person who was Black and probably Muslim. Shakespeare uses the term 'moor' and it is often combined with 'Black'.

We can infer from the source that in the Elizabethan times there was a Black presence, which the letter suggests is substantial. However, Elizabeth I claims that the population of 'our own nation' is growing and so these 'Blackmoores' should be sent out of the country. She refers to ten in particular whom she wants deported. Why does she make this instruction? This letter is written towards the end of Elizabeth's reign in 1596. The country was facing significant social and economic problems. Prices were rising, which was made worse by crop failure. Enclosures also led to higher unemployment. All these factors increased poverty, vagrancy and disease in Elizabethan society. Perhaps we can infer from the letter that Elizabeth is blaming the Black population in order to deflect from these problems. Does this mean that the Elizabethan society was an intolerant one?

Why does The National Archives have this source?

The letter appears in the records for Elizabeth I's Privy Council for 1596.

What is the context of this source?

Elizabeth I sent a second letter dated 18th July 1598 to the Mayor of London and other officials to help get 'Blackmoores' out of the country. The task of removing the 'Blackmoores' was given to a merchant called Casper van Senden of Lubeck, who had recently returned 89 English prisoners of war held in Spain and Portugal. Perhaps they were to be used in exchange or sold.

Nobody could be removed without the consent of their master, however, and there was no compensation offered, so the scheme failed. In Tudor times, Black people came to England through slavery, as servants, or as sailors. Elizabeth I had Black musicians at court. Some Black people were also free, but this is often difficult to determine in archival material.

Diverse Histories © Clare Horrie and Rachel Hillman, 2022

💡 LESSON IDEAS

ENQUIRY QUESTION
What does this source reveal about the Black presence in Elizabethan England?

Getting started

In order to encourage your students to sharpen their historical skills for the interpretation of the letter source, introduce it using the 'mystery document' approach.

Print out copies of the document or display the large image version on a whiteboard. Don't say anything about the document at this point. Tell the students they are first going to consider the source as an 'object' (how it appears, how it has been produced), and what these things can reveal, before going on to look at the contents. Give the students just five to ten minutes to make their observations.

You could use the approach below:

- *Look* at the document as an object. *Don't* read it. What do you see?
- How was it produced? (Is it typed or handwritten?)
- How is the text set out on the page? (This one is a letter, for example.)
- What does this reveal about the type of document this could be? (In this case, we can see it's a formal important letter.)
- When was it written? (Can we tell from the language?)
- Any other points to note?

Exploring further

Next, choose some key words which you think the students will be able to spot. (Use the transcript on page 24 to help you beforehand.) Display the list on the board and ask the students how many words they can spot. Highlight the words as the students find them. Then encourage students to read the document. Use the modernised transcript before offering the simplified transcript if they need more help. Alternatively, get them to underline key points in the modernised transcript to create their own 'simplified version'. Ask the students to try and make inferences based on its contents.

- Can we tell when the letter was written? (Think about the nature of the language, the ink and the overall look of the document.)
- Who has written it?
- Who are they writing to?
- What does the letter say?
- What is the voice and tone of the letter?
- What does it imply about Elizabeth I's attitude to 'Blackmoores'?

Follow-up tasks
- Ask students to write a profile or chronology of the reign of Elizabeth I.
- Encourage students to research the plot of Shakespeare's *Othello*. Teachers use extracts from the play in class to explore racial injustice and intolerance in Tudor times. Consult this article from the British Library for support: **www.bl.uk/shakespeare/articles/racism-misogyny-and-motiveless-malignity-in-othello**
- Teachers will find ten highly illuminating case studies they may wish to share with students in Miranda Kaufman's book *Black Tudors: The Untold Story*.

Lesson 3
Black Tudors

TRANSCRIPT

Modernised transcript

An open letter to the Lord Mayor of London and the aldermen his brethren. And to all other Mayors, Sheriffs etc. Her Majesty understanding that there are of late divers Blackmoores brought into the Realm, of which kind of people there are already here too many, considering how God hath blessed this land with great increase of people of our own Nation as any country in the world. Whereof many for want of service and means to set them on work fall to idleness and to great extremity. Her Majesty's pleasure therefore is that those kind of people should be sent forth of the land. And for that purpose there is direction given to this bearer Edward Banes to take those Blackmoores that in this last voyage under Sir Thomas Baskervile were brought into this realm to the number of ten, to be transported by him out of the Realm. Wherein we require you to be aiding and assisting unto him as he shall have occasion and thereof not to fail.

Simplified transcript

To the Lord Mayor of London and his officers and all other mayors and sheriffs in the country. Her Majesty is aware that a lot of Blackmoores have been brought to this country where many live already, at a time when God has seen it fit to increase the size of our own population. Many of them need work but without it turn to idleness and poverty. It is her Majesty's wish that these kind of people should be sent [deported] out of the country. Edward Banes is to transport out of the country 10 Blackmoores brought into the country by Sir Thomas Baskerville. Everyone is to help him ensure that this does not fail to happen.

LESSON 4

JEAN BARBOT

CONNECTION TO THE CURRICULUM

The development of Church, state and society in Britain 1509–1745

Aim: To find out about the people and societies of West Africa in the late seventeenth century.

Historical figure: Jean Barbot (1655–1712)

Source: An interview with the King of Sestro (ADM 7/830A, f.96)

TEACHER'S NOTES

What is this source?
This document is taken from files held within the Admiralty records. These records contain information relating to the Royal Navy and associated naval forces.

What can we infer from this source?
This document has been hand-drawn in black ink. It shows a group of African people sitting in a semi-circle within a straw-roofed building. There are two small windows on the back wall of the building and what looks like a type of rush-matting on the floor. The seated men are resting on mats and are wearing long, light-coloured robes.

In the centre of these men sits a figure dressed differently to the others. This man is wearing a headpiece made of straw, similar to a crown, decorated with what look like goats' horns, suggesting that he is of a much higher status than the men seated around him. There are further figures seated in front of this important man, in what appears to be European dress. They are wearing hose, hats, leather boots and tunics, with long hairstyles and swords at their waists. One of the European figures is standing, and is accompanied by two African men who are holding spears. This suggests they could be guards.

Items have been placed on the floor of the room: two large bottles, a basket of dead birds and a tablet-picture with two figures carefully engraved. There is an open fire burning.

The scene appears to be a meeting between the important African man of status and his advisers, and the European men. The style of the Europeans' dress suggests that this document could be dated around the seventeenth century.

Why does The National Archives have this source?
This document is held within files relating to the Admiralty.

What is the context of this source?
This image was drawn by Jean Barbot. Between 1682 and 1687, Barbot worked as a commercial agent on a number of French slave-trading voyages to the Gold Coast (modern Ghana) in West Africa. This meant that he was trading for gold and ivory amongst other items and supplies.

During his travels, Barbot kept journals with detailed descriptions and illustrations of his observations, including scenes from African life, plants and flowers, views of the coastline and forts built by the Europeans. Alongside this, Barbot wrote about the transatlantic slave trade, describing how it was carried out and who was involved. For many years, his writing was considered an important source. However, later research revealed that he did not experience or witness everything he wrote about, but drew detail from other writers such as Olfert Dapper (1639–89).

The scene in the source shows Barbot meeting with the King of Sestro (in modern Liberia) to trade for ivory. Barbot is the European figure seated next to the King.

💡 LESSON IDEAS

ENQUIRY QUESTION
What does this document reveal about the people and societies of West Africa in the late seventeenth century?

Getting started

This document could be used as contextual material for teaching about West Africa and the transatlantic slave trade. Further information and sources can be found at: **www.nationalarchives.gov.uk/pathways/blackhistory/africa_caribbean/africa_trade.htm**

Begin by asking students to describe everything they can see in the picture, and then start to make inferences. For example:

- Where is the picture set?
- Who are the people and how are they dressed?
- What is happening?
- Can you suggest a date or time period for the document?
- Why do you think this document has been created?

Exploring further

Explain the provenance of the image and ask students to consider what this picture reveals about people and society in West Africa at this time. Are there parallels with European society in the late 1600s?

Discuss the perspective that this source has been drawn from. Jean Barbot was a slave trader. What other types of documents could students use to find out more about West Africa at this time?

Follow-up tasks

- Introduce students to information about West Africa before the Europeans using the Black Presence website: **www.nationalarchives.gov.uk/pathways/blackhistory/africa_caribbean/west_africa.htm**. There is so much to explore, from the ancient kingdom of Ghana, which flourished from at least the eighth century AD, to the Mali empire, a confederation of states that governed much of modern Senegal and Mali in the Middle Ages.

PART 2

IDEAS, POLITICAL POWER

INDUSTRY AND EMPIRE:

BRITAIN, 1745–1901

LESSON 5

SEVENTEENTH-CENTURY JAMAICA

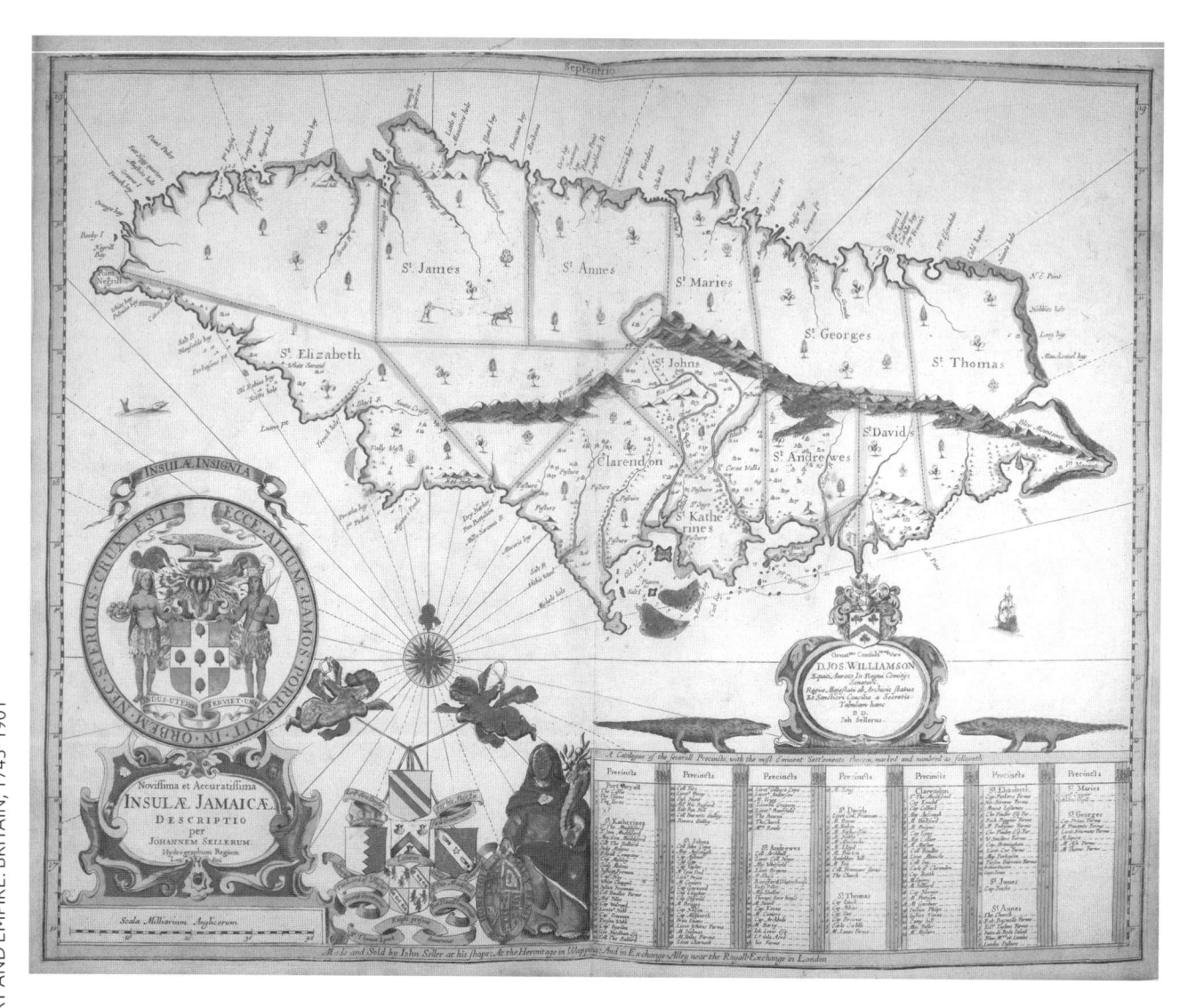

CONNECTION TO THE CURRICULUM

Ideas, political power, industry and empire: Britain, 1745–1901

Aim: To find out about Jamaica in the late seventeenth century.

Historical event: Jamaica as part of the British Empire

Source: Map of Jamaica (FO 925/4111 f.34)

TEACHER'S NOTES

What is this source?

This is a map of Jamaica from a Foreign Office file. It is dated 1698 and shows Jamaica when it was under British colonial rule during the reign of William III.

What can we infer from this source?

This map has been beautifully created; it shows illustrations of trees and plants, along with rivers and hills. In the interior of the island we can see mountainous areas, and towards the top of the map there are parishes that appear to be less densely settled. On the opposite side of the island, much of the land is being used for pasture and the raising of livestock, suggesting more people live there. *Port Royall* can also be seen, indicating an area of shipping and commerce.

Although the cartographer has labelled the different parishes on the map, he hasn't included detail such as the names of towns or villages. However, he has named each place along the sea coast; perhaps the map's primary purpose is to reveal information about the coastline.

Below the map of Jamaica, we can see the Jamaican coat of arms. The name of the cartographer (the person who created this map), is written in Latin – Johannem Sellerum or John Seller.

We can also see the names of the different governors of Jamaica along with two angels and the figure of a seated man, holding what appear to be Lignum Vitai flowers (the national flower of Jamaica). The Governor General acts as the monarch's representative in Jamaica.

On the right-hand bottom corner of the map, John Seller has listed 'A catalogue of the several precincts with the most eminent settlements', which includes the names of people and significant buildings in certain parishes. This also tells us that earlier inferences about the more densely settled areas of the island are accurate, as parishes such as St. James and St. Anne's have fewer people listed.

Why does The National Archives have this source?

This document is held within a Foreign Office file. It comes from a larger document called *Atlaticus Maritimus* containing charts and maps detailing the sea coasts.

What is the context of this source?

This map shows Jamaica in 1698, over 40 years after the British had taken the island from the Spanish and declared it part of the British Empire. Jamaica first became an imperial colony of the Spanish in 1509 when the indigenous Arawak people were driven from their homes and enslaved by the Spanish explorers.

By the end of the seventeenth century, many escaped slaves were joining the indigenous Taino people in the mountainous interior of Jamaica, and creating a new society known as the Maroons. The Maroons resisted and fought back against British colonial rule. In 1739, the Maroons and the British agreed a peace settlement, in which the Maroons' land and freedom were recognised.

Jamaica did not gain independence from the British until 1962.

💡 LESSON IDEAS

ENQUIRY QUESTION
What does this map reveal about the island of Jamaica in 1698?

Getting started

Use this document as part of a series of lessons about places under British colonial rule to provide context, background information and understanding to 'ideas, political power, industry and empire: Britain, 1745–1901'.

To introduce the source, take a 'mystery document' approach and don't tell students anything about the document before you reveal it to them. Give them five minutes to explore the map and think about the following questions:

- What can you see?
- Which place does this map show?
- Why has the map been produced? Why do you think this?
- What does the map reveal about this place and its relationship to the British Empire?

Exploring further

Using the teacher's notes on the previous page, confirm that this is a map of Jamaica and tell the students more about the colonisation of Jamaica in the 1500s and 1600s. Link this to your learning about the transatlantic slave trade. What other documents could students look at to give them an idea of what British colonial rule was like for both the enslaved and indigenous people of Jamaica?

Introduce the Maroons and explore how they resisted and fought back against British rule. Do the students know any other stories of resistance to enslavement? You could use the resources on BBC Bitesize to explore this topic further: **www.bbc.co.uk/bitesize/guides/z732pv4/revision**

Revolts that took place in Jamaica include Tacky's Revolt in 1760 and the rebellion in Jamaica in 1831, where 20,000 people seized control in the north-west of the island and set planters' houses alight.

Follow-up tasks

- Introduce students to Catherine Johnson's book *Queen of Freedom: Defending Jamaica*. This retells the story of Queen Nanny, a woman who masterminded a slave resistance against the British in eighteenth-century Jamaica.
- Introduce students to *Cane Warriors* by Alex Wheatle, which tells the story of the 1760 Jamaican rebellion through the fictional character of 14-year-old Moa.

LESSON 6

BLACK GEORGIANS

TASTE IN HIGH LIFE.

CONNECTION TO THE CURRICULUM

Ideas, political power, industry and empire: Britain, 1745–1901

Aim: To discover how Black Georgians were represented by William Hogarth.

Historical figure: William Hogarth (1697–1764)

Source: Print of a painting by William Hogarth, British Museum (1862.1011.409)

© The Trustees of the British Museum

TEACHER'S NOTES

What is this source?

This is a print made from a painting by William Hogarth. The caption reads: 'Painted by Mr. Hogarth. Sold by Mr. Jarvis in Bedford Court Covent Garden. Price 6d. Published May 24th. According to Act of Parliament, 1746.'

What can we infer from this source?

Hogarth's print shows an expensively furnished interior with an elderly lady wearing an enormous hooped petticoat talking to an extravagantly dressed gentleman who is examining a tiny tea cup. On the left, a fashionable young lady pats a Black page boy under the chin. In the foreground, a monkey wearing an oversized coat and a three-cornered hat reads a menu beginning 'Pour Dinner/Cox Combs...' On the back wall there are pictures, including one labelled 'Insects' and another showing a statue of Venus with a hooped petticoat and stays. Another picture called 'Exotics' shows a collection of hair accessories.

Hogarth is attacking the stupidity of the upper classes in their desire to wear fashionable clothes, no matter how uncomfortable, or purchase exquisite *objets d'art*, but also to own enslaved domestic servants. In this picture, the child is depicted as an object of fashion, similar to other popular consumer products of slavery, like tea, coffee, chocolate, sugar or tobacco, all popular in the Georgian period.

Tea services imported from China were growing in popularity at the start of the eighteenth century. People took sugar with their tea so often Black servants were depicted in scenes showing tea making. The picture reflects that slavery existed in England, not just in colonial plantations. The world of the wealthy aristocrat was often embedded in the system of slavery and economic exploitation. Indeed, both Hogarth's painted narrative series, *A Harlot's Progress* and *A Rake's Progress*, were purchased by William Beckford of Fonthill, the art collector and novelist who owned extensive plantations in Jamaica.

Why does the British Museum have it?

The print was acquired by the British Museum in 1868 but is not currently on display.

What is the context of this source?

It is difficult to provide exact statistics for the size of the Black population of Georgian Britain. It was estimated, according to David Olusoga, to be about 15,000 in 1772, which included London and the ports of Bristol and Liverpool associated with the expansion of the slave trade.

Some plantation owners brought enslaved people to work for them in England. They had no rights and were treated as property, merely representing the fashionable tastes of their owners, as shown in Hogarth's print. However, it's important to note that not all Black people living in Britain were enslaved as unpaid domestic servants. For example, Francis Barber (1735–1801) was a Jamaican man who was secretary to Dr Samuel Johnson. Johnson left Barber £70 a year, books and a watch in his will. Ignatius Sancho (1729–1780), who was a former butler to the Montagu family, later became an author of a collection of letters on slavery and empire published in 1782.

💡 LESSON IDEAS

ENQUIRY QUESTION
What does this source reveal about Black Georgians?

Getting started

Use this lesson as part of a scheme of work exploring the history of the British Empire and the transatlantic slave trade, building on Lessons 5 and 8.

In order to encourage your students to develop their observational skills for the interpretation of this source, introduce it using the 'five-second rule'. Give the class just five seconds to look at the source on a whiteboard or printout. Ask them to remember anything they notice. Repeat this a second time, but give them ten seconds to view the source. What else have they noticed?

Exploring further

Now reveal the image for five to ten minutes and ask students to jot down all the points they can make about the source. Next ask students to share their thoughts in a discussion to answer the enquiry question: What does this source reveal about Black Georgians?

Use these suggested prompt questions for discussion:

- Can you describe the scene?
- Why is the painting called *Taste in High Life*?
- What is the possible message of the picture?
- Why is the artist showing an enslaved boy? How is he dressed?
- What do you notice about the other people in the picture?

6. What do you think the artwork on the wall behind the people suggests?
7. Are there any limitations to this historical source?
8. Can you describe the style of the picture?
9. How can we date it as 'Georgian'?
10. What does the image reveal which a written document might not?
11. What other sources would help us to find out more about the enslaved in Britain?

Follow-up tasks

- Ask students to research and collate other works by Hogarth which have depicted Black people enslaved as domestic servants. Students create their own captions to explain their interpretation of each source. You could consult *Hogarth: World of Art* by David Bindman to support this task. This useful book includes a discussion of Hogarth's many representations of African people in eighteenth-century Britain and contains a huge number of images of his work.
- For much more on Black Georgians, consult Chapter 3 in *Black and British: A Forgotten History* by David Olusoga. This book provides a lot of detail about Black people living in Britain in this period and refers to many primary sources.

LESSON 7

THE 'BLACK POOR'

An Alphabetical List of the Black People who have received the Bounty from Government

1	John Adams	31	Abram Allison
2	George Adams & Child	32	Samuel Adamson
3	John Ashfield	33	John Aberdeen
4	James Anderson	34	Ann Allamaze
5	Arch.d Anderson	35	Robert Ashfield
6	John Albert	36	Jack Andrew
7	William Anderson	37	John Ashfield
8	Ebenez.r Anderson	38	Jack Anthony
9	Tom Agnew	39	Joseph Antoney
10	Thomas Ashworth	40	John Antoney
11	James Annison	41	John Brown
12	Thomas Adams	42	Joseph Brown
13	John Anthony	43	Thomas Bruce
14	Sylva Allen	44	John Beckett
15	James Atkins	45	William Barnes
16	Samuel Allen	46	George Broomfield
17	Thomas Amsley	47	William Bird
18	Teirew Ambo	48	Benj.n Brown
19	Timothy Allenby	49	Joseph Barley
20	Joseph Allamaze	50	William Blue
21	Harry Armstrong	51	George Brown
22	Joshua Allamaze	52	Joshua Brown
23	Henry Alexander	53	Aaron Brooks
24	Daniel Allington	54	John Bell
25	Jacob Annand	55	Peter Bristow
26	Charles Adams	56	John Brandy
27	Jack Anthony	57	Jacob Boss
28	Joseph Anderson	58	David Brown
29	Syllavo Augustavus	59	Anth.y Burgess
30	John Adams	60	Richard Bristow

CONNECTION TO THE CURRICULUM

The development of Church, state and society in Britain 1509–1745

Aim: To find out about society in London in the late 1780s.

Historical event: Creation of the 'Committee for the Relief of the Black Poor'

Source: An alphabetical list of the Black People who have received the bounty from government (T 1/638 (f.240))

PART 2 IDEAS, POLITICAL POWER, INDUSTRY AND EMPIRE: BRITAIN, 1745–1901

📖 TEACHER'S NOTES

What is this source?

This is an extract from a record held within Treasury files, dated 1786.

What can we infer from this source?

This document has been handwritten and only lists people's surnames beginning with A or B, suggesting that it is the front page from a much longer document.

The style of handwriting is not contemporary and the title 'Bounty from Government' also suggests that the document dates from an earlier time. 'Bounty' implies some type of payment that the government were giving to those described as Black.

All of the names listed are male, so perhaps the women's names have been listed on a different page. Or perhaps women weren't given the money directly, but it was given to a male relative or guardian. There is only one man listed with a child, 'George Adams and child'; this might be a rare occurrence, or there may be further examples on subsequent pages. On this page alone there are 60 names, all in receipt of this government money. Most of the names appear British in origin, e.g. 'John' and 'George', but there are a few names that would have been less common in Britain at the time, e.g. 'Ebinoy' and 'Silva'.

There is no indication of place on this document.

Why does The National Archives have this source?

This document is held within Treasury files dated 1782–1837. The Treasury is responsible for managing the finances of government.

What is the context of this source?

This document is dated 1786 and was created after the American War of Independence. The number of Black people in London at this time increased, but there was a history of Black people in the city before this date.

'Black Poor' was the collective name given to people who were receiving some kind of poor relief and were of Black descent. They had many different backgrounds; some had been brought to London as part of the transatlantic slave trade, either as enslaved people or indentured servants on ships, others had run away from slave owners. Lord Dunmore's Declaration in 1775, 'freeing all slaves and indentured servants willing to fight for the British', meant that thousands of enslaved people who had fought on the side of the British subsequently found their way to London as freemen. There were also Black sailors serving in the Royal Navy and on merchant ships at this time. In 1731, the Corporation of London had barred all Black men from seeking apprenticeships, blocking their way to skilled trades.

By 1786, there were many Black people receiving financial assistance, with philanthropists contributing to a charitable organisation 'The Committee for the Relief of the Black Poor'. It organised regular alms giving, along with a sick house for those who needed medical attention. Government officials also became involved when it was proposed that the Committee could resettle the Black Poor in Sierra Leone. Seeing an opportunity to remove the 'Black Poor' from London streets, the government gave their support. Many Black people did not want to leave Britain, so payments were only made to those who agreed to go to Sierra Leone.

Diverse Histories © Clare Horrie and Rachel Hillman, 2022

LESSON IDEAS

ENQUIRY QUESTION
What does this document reveal about society in eighteenth-century London?

Getting started

Use this document to help explore the presence of Black people living in eighteenth-century London.

To get started, remove the title of the document and take a 'mystery document' approach with the students. Don't tell them anything about the document before you share it with them. Give them five minutes to explore the document and think about the following questions:

- What type of document do you think it is?
- When do you think it was created?
- Can you read any of the names?
- Who do you think these people are?

Discuss their findings before revealing the title of the document. How have their initial inferences changed?

Exploring further

Host a class discussion based on the following enquiry question: based on their findings in the starter activity, what do the students think the document can now reveal about society in London at this time? Think particularly about what this document reveals about race relations in Britain in the late 1700s. Use the teacher's notes to disclose information about the source and its context as and when appropriate during the discussion.

Follow-up tasks

- Introduce students to more information about the 'Sierra Leone Scheme' by visiting websites such as 'Black Presence' and 'Find my Past': **www.nationalarchives.gov.uk/pathways/blackhistory/work_community/poor.htm www.findmypast.co.uk/blog/history/sierra-leone**
- Encourage students to research some of those who opposed the Sierra Leone Scheme, such as Olaudah Equiano (also known as Gustavus Vassa) and Ottobah Cugoano. What were their reasons for opposing the scheme? Ask the students to write a persuasive speech for one of these historical figures outlining their arguments against the scheme. (To discover more about Olaudah Equiano, see Lesson 10.)

LESSON 8

SLAVERY IN BERMUDA

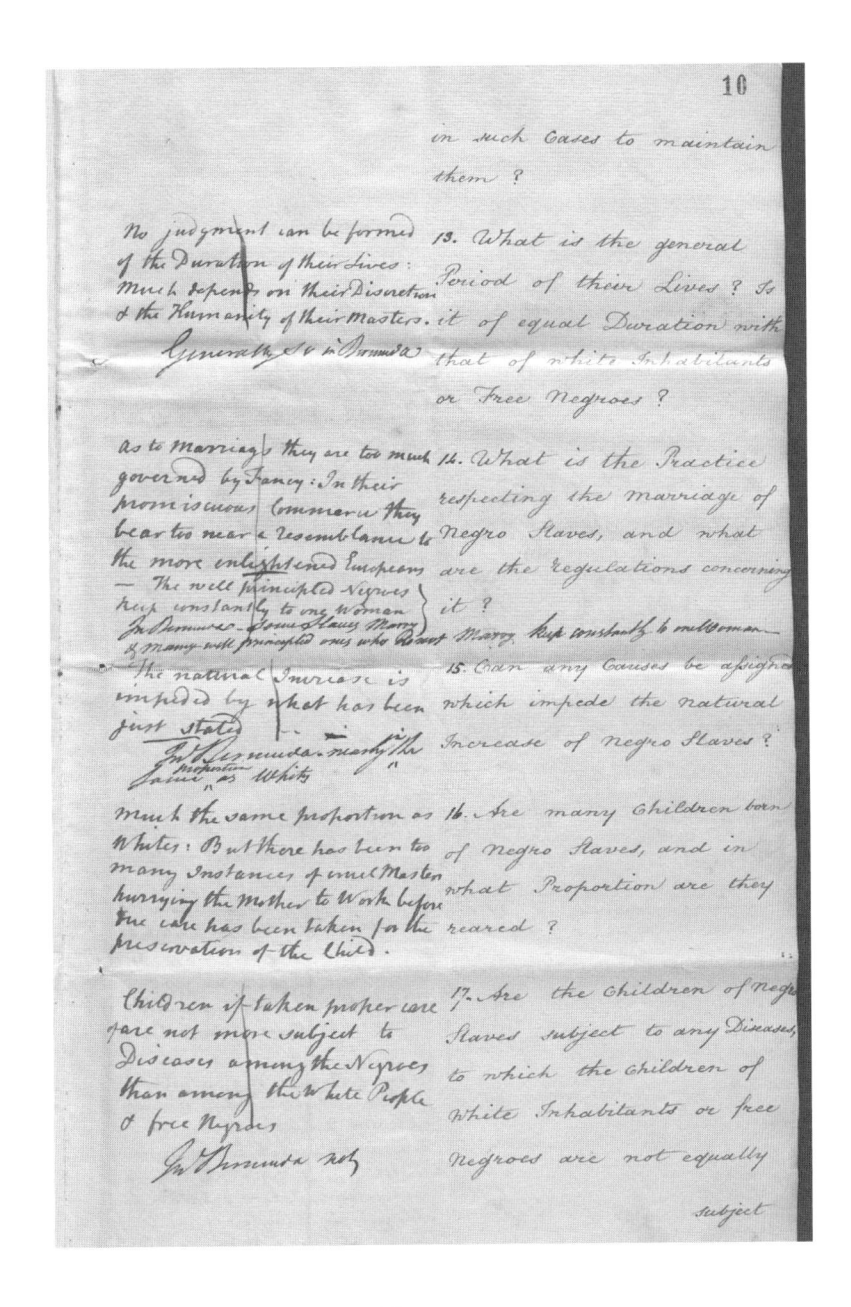

CONNECTION TO THE CURRICULUM

Ideas, political power, industry and empire: Britain, 1745–1901

Aim: To explore conditions of the enslaved in eighteenth-century Bermuda.

Historical event: Slavery in Bermuda

Source: A questionnaire about conditions for the enslaved (CO 37/38 f.10)

Caution: This source contains language that is inappropriate and unacceptable today.

TEACHER'S NOTES

What is this source?
This is a page from a questionnaire about conditions for the enslaved, dated 1786.

What can we infer from this source?
This document shows the treatment of the enslaved in Bermuda. We can infer that the colonial authorities were keen to make the most profit from 'the trade' and highlights some of the risks they considered possible.

The extract is part of a questionnaire designed to gather information about the enslaved on the island and in British colonies in the West Indies. We can tell this by the numbering of the questions.

The document consists of some notes on the left that respond to a question on the right. It is not clear if 'Mr Jennings' wrote the questionnaire and his notes were used to form the questions, or if he was providing answers to the questions. The nature and tone of all the questions are highly offensive and inappropriate to us today. Their purpose is to get as much detailed information as possible. The words 'Negro' and 'slave' are used interchangeably for the enslaved. 'Free Negroes' were not enslaved and might be found in the British colonies in North America.

Question 13 implies that the enslaved were seen as no more than chattels and those who lived longest were economically more valuable to the masters. Other questions relate to marriage and children. According to the 'notes', some of the enslaved had relationships like 'enlightened Europeans', possibly a reference to the Enlightenment in Europe during the eighteenth century.

Insight into the lives of the enslaved is given through Jennings' notes about the children born to enslaved women. He says that some women were forced into going back to work too soon by 'cruel masters' without care for the 'preservation of the child'. The last question about disease amongst children implies concern about the potential loss of income and threat to the White community.

Why does The National Archives have this source?
The document is held within the Colonial Office collection, which includes correspondence sent out by the Colonial Office to governments and officials.

What is the context?
Bermuda was colonised by the British and settled by the British Virginia Company in 1609. The colony's labour force consisted of indentured servants, Irish and Scottish prisoners, and rising numbers of enslaved Africans and Native Americans who had been transported to Bermuda. It was the first colony to import enslaved Africans.

Bermuda was different to other English colonies. It was not in the Caribbean and it did not develop a plantation system, for example, like Barbados, a slave society. Instead it developed a maritime economy with slaves based on shipbuilding, slave trading, transporting of goods, salvaging shipwrecks or piracy.

There are a total of 35 questions covering the legal power of masters, the legal protection slaves have, the 'maintenance' cost of a slave, whether slaves go to church and the amount of land in cultivation.

💡 LESSON IDEAS

ENQUIRY QUESTION
What does this source reveal about slavery in Bermuda?

Getting started

Use this lesson, a case study on Bermuda, as part of a scheme of work exploring the history of the British Empire and the transatlantic slave trade.

Before reading the source, it is important to check the students understand the following words. If not, offer them definitions:

- discretion
- duration
- assigned
- impeded
- promiscuous
- imputed
- 'free Negroes'.

Now read and discuss the source using the prompt questions below to help. You will likely need to hand out a copy of the transcript on page 42, but ask the students to try to identify words or phrases on the original source initially.

- Describe the look of the document.
- What type of document is it?
- Do you know anything about the author or creator?
- When was it written or produced?
- Why was it written or produced?

Exploring further

Now move into a wider class discussion about what the source reveals about slavery in (a) Bermuda (b) other British colonies. What values or attitudes does the content of the source reflect?

Ask the students to come up with six to ten additional questions for the 'questionnaire' to be completed by owners of the enslaved for the colonial authorities. Discuss these additional questions in class, encouraging the students to give reasons for their selections.

Follow-up tasks

- Draw a map to show the location of Bermuda and include Britain's other colonies in the Caribbean in the eighteenth century.
- Write a profile of Mary Prince (c.1788–c.1833), a British abolitionist and autobiographer who was born in Bermuda to an enslaved family of African descent. Her book was the first ever female account of enslavement. From 2020, Mary Prince Day is a public holiday in Bermuda. The profile could be recorded as an audio clip or a video as an alternative.
- Explore the second lesson on slavery (Lesson 9), which covers the Resistance of the enslaved.

LESSON 8
Slavery in Bermuda

TRANSCRIPT

No Judgement can be formed of the Duration of their lives: Much depends on their Discretion and Humanity of their Masters. Generally so in Bermuda.	13. What is the general Period of their lives? Is it of equal Duration with that of White inhabitants or Free Negroes?
As to marriages, they are too much governed by Fancy: In their promiscuous commerce they bear too near a resemblance to the more enlightened Europeans. The well-principled Negroes keep constantly to one woman. In Bermuda some slaves marry & many well principled ones who resist marriage keep constantly to one woman.	14. What is the Practice respecting the marriage of Negro slaves, and what are the regulations concerning it?
The natural increase is impeded by what has been just stated. In Bermuda in the same proportion as whites.	15. Can any causes be assigned which impede the natural increase of Negro slaves?
Much the same proportion as the whites. But there has been too many instances of cruel masters hurrying the mother to work before the case has been taken for the preservation of the child.	16. Are many children born of Negro slaves, and in what proportion are they reared?
Children if taken proper care of are not more subject to Diseases among the Negroes than among the White People or Free Negroes. In Bermuda not.	17. Are the children of Negro slaves subject to any Diseases to which the children of white inhabitants or free Negroes are not equally subject, [and what cause is it to be imputed?]

LESSON 9

RESISTANCE TO SLAVERY IN ST VINCENT

> RUN-AWAY,
> ON Sunday last, Three NEW NEGROES, two men named YORICK and CATO, and a girl named FATIMA, they pretend to be brothers and sister, and are all of the Mendingo or Soroco nation; had on red jackets, bound hats, and short Osnaburg trousers, remarkably black, but no particular marks. YORICK has a small sore on his shin, speaks a few words and will be able to tell where he belongs. Whoever takes up said Negroes and sends them to their owner, shall receive a suitable reward.
> JOHN MASSEY.
> Biabou, Nov. 4, 1786.

> Marshal's-Office, in Kingstown, November 11, 1786.
> NOTICE is hereby given, that is now confined the Common Goal of this Island, a Negroe Girl, about 5 feet high, of the Moco Nation, taken up the 6th instant on Sion Hill, and sent to Gaol by note from Mr. Sim.
> If not claimed in due time, she will be sold to pay her gaol fees and expences of taking up.
> GILBERT HILLOCK,
> Dep. Pro. Marshal.

> **CONNECTION TO THE CURRICULUM**
> Ideas, political power, industry and empire: Britain, 1745–1901
> **Aim:** Explore examples of resistance to slavery in St Vincent in the Caribbean.
> **Historical event:** Resistance of the enslaved
> **Source:** Two extracts from *The Royal St Vincent's Gazette and General Advertiser* (CO 7/1)
> **Caution:** This source contains language that is inappropriate and unacceptable today.

TEACHER'S NOTES

What is this source?
These are two extracts from a page of *The Royal St Vincent's Gazette and General Advertiser*, dated Saturday 11th November 1786.

What can we infer from this source?
Each of these short advertisements offers reward for escaped enslaved men and children. They represent examples of resistance by the enslaved. The enslaved perhaps have been recently acquired and are wishing to make an early escape – in the first advert they are described as 'New Negroes'.

In the first advertisement by John Massey, the enslaved are described according to their alleged names. 'Cato' would seem to be the name given by the master after the Roman historian and 'Yorick' may be after the character in Shakespeare's *Hamlet*. The girl has been named 'Fatima'. This renaming is a sign of the master asserting his ownership and his wish to eradicate any sense of personal identity.

Their outfits are described as 'red jackets and bound hats', a form of livery to show the status of the master and the badge of the enslaved. This could represent a significant financial loss to the master as well as the loss of the enslaved themselves. They are also wearing trousers made from 'Oznabrig', a textile woven from hemp or flax. This was an unbleached, cheap fabric that was imported in vast quantities to clothe the enslaved. 'Yoricke' has a sore on his shin. Is this due to mistreatment, from wearing shackles, or due to malnutrition? These people are being treated as if chattels or livestock and their loss is advertised in the same way.

The second advertisement by Gilbert Hillock, the Deputy Provincial Marshal, states that a 'Negroe girl, about five foot high' is in gaol until she is claimed, otherwise she will be sold to pay for her gaol fees. This reflects the cruel system of slavery and it is shocking that the judicial system acts to perpetuate it.

Why does The National Archives have this source?
The newspaper is held within the Colonial Office collection, which includes correspondence sent out by the Colonial Office to governments, officials and individuals between the seventeenth century and 1926.

What is the context of this source?
In 1763 Britain gained control of St Vincent by the Treaty of Paris. In 1779 the island was taken by the French, but was regained by the British in 1783. The island of St Vincent imported thousands of African slaves until 1807 and both Englishmen and Scotsmen set up sugar plantations as part of the economy of slavery within the British Empire.

These 'reward' notices for the return of missing enslaved men and children sit alongside other advertisements for the sale of mules or imported goods from England, including Yorkshire ham, cheese, wine and 'some fashionable buttons'. There are details about the auction of a sugar plantation and a story taken from the *London Gazette* about the King and Queen making a visit to Oxford.

These advertisements were a regular feature in other newspapers, such as *The Barbados Mercury*, and reveal that Africans often showed their resistance by running away from the plantations.

💡 LESSON IDEAS

ENQUIRY QUESTION
What does this source reveal about how the enslaved resisted the system of slavery?

Getting started

Use this lesson as part of a scheme of work exploring the history of the British Empire and the transatlantic slave trade. Build on the work covered in Lessons 8 and 12 relating to the history of slavery.

Work with the students to establish what this source is about and what they can infer about the treatment of enslaved people and how they might try to resist the system of slavery. Explain to the students that resistance among enslaved Africans began the moment they were captured and took many different forms. Discuss different forms of resistance by the enslaved, for example: running away; speaking privately in their own languages; performing African rituals and religious practice; damaging tools. However, rebellion was the most direct form of resistance.

Exploring further

Explore rebellion as a form of resistance to slavery. Introduce the students to Bussa's rebellion in Barbados in 1816 as an example of this. The rebellion was led by Bussa, who was an African-born enslaved man and a ranger on a plantation in St Philip. As a ranger, Bussa would have travelled to different estates in the area, enabling him to plan an uprising with enslaved men and women from these estates.

Explore the original primary sources available on The National Archives website with the students to find out what happened during the rebellion: **www.nationalarchives.gov.uk/education/resources/bussas-rebellion**.

Ask the students to read the sources to find out the answers to the following questions, either individually or in pairs:

- How did the enslaved show their rebellion? (They set fire to canes, plantations and houses, and scattered furniture, rum, sugar, wine, corn and other foods in the roads and fields.)
- How did the British authorities respond to the rebellion? (They sent military troops to the rebellion to seize control.)
- How many troops were deployed to control the rebellion? (A total of 650 men from three different regiments.)
- How many people died on both sides? (50 enslaved people were killed and 70 were executed during the battle. In comparison, one Black solider and one White civilian died in the fighting.)

Encourage the students to share their answers in a final class discussion.

Follow-up tasks

- Write an account or chronology of the most successful rebellion of the enslaved, led by the Maroons in Haiti in 1791.
- Students can create a profile about the significance of Sam Sharpe in the history of slavery. Sharpe was an enslaved Jamaican who led the 1831–1832 Baptist War slave rebellion in Jamaica, which was a key event in the abolition movement. Ask students to research Sharpe, create a timeline of his life and discuss his role in the Baptist War slave rebellion. They can share their profile in written, audio or video format.

LESSON 10

OLAUDAH EQUIANO

CONNECTION TO THE CURRICULUM

Ideas, political power, industry and empire: Britain, 1745–1901

Aim: To find out about the life of Olaudah Equiano, also known as Gustavus Vassa.
Historical figure: Olaudah Equiano (c. 1745–1797), also known as Gustavus Vassa
Source: Extract of a letter from Olaudah Equiano (Gustavus Vassa) (TS 24/12/2)

TEACHER'S NOTES

What is this source?

This is an extract from a letter written by Olaudah Equiano (Gustavus Vassa), 'The African'. Equiano is writing to Thomas Hardy in 1792.

What can we infer from this source?

This letter extract is handwritten and has been signed 'Gustavus Vassa, The African'. The handwriting, the language used and the appearance of the document reveal that it is not a contemporary letter. We can infer that the writer is religious, as he makes reference to God and Jesus Christ, and refers to himself as a Christian.

Equiano also seems to care for the person he is writing to, as he hopes that God will keep them both from the 'attachment to this evil world and the things of it'. This suggests that he has seen or experienced some kind of terrible hardship or trauma, and that this has fundamentally shaped the way he views the world. To sign the letter with both the name Gustavus Vassa and then the title of 'The African' also reveals something else significant about him. Equiano is proud of his heritage and where he has come from, using this as a way to positively identify himself.

Why does The National Archives have this source?

This letter comes from the Treasury Solicitor's papers, acting on behalf of the Treasury and other government departments in legal matters. These papers are referred to as miscellaneous papers on sedition cases. Sedition refers to actions or speech inciting people to rebel against the government.

What is the context of this source?

Gustavus Vassa was the name that the writer of this letter was given when he was enslaved at the age of 11. His real name was Olaudah Equiano, and he was born in the Eboe region – now known as Nigeria. He was transported on a slave ship from his homeland to Barbados, and then onto Virginia in North America, where he was bought by a man called Michael Pascal, a Lieutenant in the Royal Navy. Equiano was renamed by Pascal and given the name of Gustavus Vassa, a former king of Sweden from the sixteenth century.

Relatives of Pascal taught Equiano how to read and write, and taught him about Christianity. Equiano was baptised in 1759.

Equiano traded well and saved his money carefully. Eventually he had enough money to buy his freedom from his final master, an English merchant in Montserrat. In 1766, he paid £40 for his freedom and went on to marry an English woman, Susannah Cullen, in 1792.

As a freed man, Equiano supported the British Abolitionist Movement and became active among the leaders of the anti-slave trade movement. He wrote his autobiography in 1789, *The Interesting Narrative of the Life of Olaudah Equiano*, one of the very first books published in Europe written by a Black African writer. It told of the horrors of slavery, and helped to move public opinion against enslavement and the slave trade, which contributed to the abolition of the British Slave Trade Act in 1807.

Equiano knew Thomas Hardy, the founder of the London Corresponding Society. In 1790, Equiano spent time staying with Hardy and his wife in London.

LESSON IDEAS

ENQUIRY QUESTION
What does this document reveal about the life of Olaudah Equiano?

Getting started

Use this document to introduce students to Olaudah Equiano (Gustuvas Vassa). Suggested prompt questions for discussion:

- Why has Equiano signed the letter 'The African'? What does this reveal about how he views his heritage?
- Why do you think Equiano describes the world as 'evil'? What do you think he has endured?
- Why do you think Equiano considers it important to refer to himself as a Christian? What role do you think religion might have played in his life?

Use the teacher's notes to draw out important points and to share the key information about Olaudah Equiano's life.

Exploring further

As a class, investigate the lives of other Black writers and campaigners whose work helped to abolish slavery in Britain, such as Mary Prince and Ignatius Sancho. Use the following notes as a starting point and ask students to analyse quotes from these writers' works.

Mary Prince

Born in Bermuda to an enslaved family of African descent, Mary Prince escaped when slave owner John Adams Wood travelled to London in 1828 and brought Prince with him as a servant. Prince wrote her autobiography, which was published in 1831 and included many horrific experiences she'd had as a slave. The text was the first narrative by a female slave from the British Caribbean. In the book, she writes about her purpose in sharing her experiences:

'Oh the horrors of slavery! – How the thought of it pains my heart! But the truth ought to be told of it; and what my eyes have seen I think it is my duty to relate; for few people in England know what slavery is. I have been a slave – I have felt what a slave feels, and I know what a slave knows; and I would have all the good people in England to know it too, that they may break our chains, and set us free.'

For more information about Mary Prince, visit: **www.maryprince.org**.

Ignatius Sancho

Ignatius Sancho came to England in 1731 at the age of two. He was born into slavery but spent much of his adult life as a free man. He was employed in the household of the Duke of Montagu before becoming a shopkeeper in Mayfair in the 1770s. Sancho was known as a connoisseur of the arts and moved in literary and artistic circles. Published posthumously in 1782, his letters describe the commercial greed of the slave trade: 'the grand object of English navigators, indeed of all Christian navigators, is money - money - money . . .'. The British Library has more information: **www.bl.uk/people/ignatius-sancho**.

Follow-up tasks

- Introduce students to Equiano's autobiography, *The Interesting Narrative of the Life of Olaudah Equiano*.
- Students could find out more about transatlantic slavery at: **www.understandingslavery.com**.

Diverse Histories © Clare Horrie and Rachel Hillman, 2022

LESSON 11

WILLIAM DAVIDSON

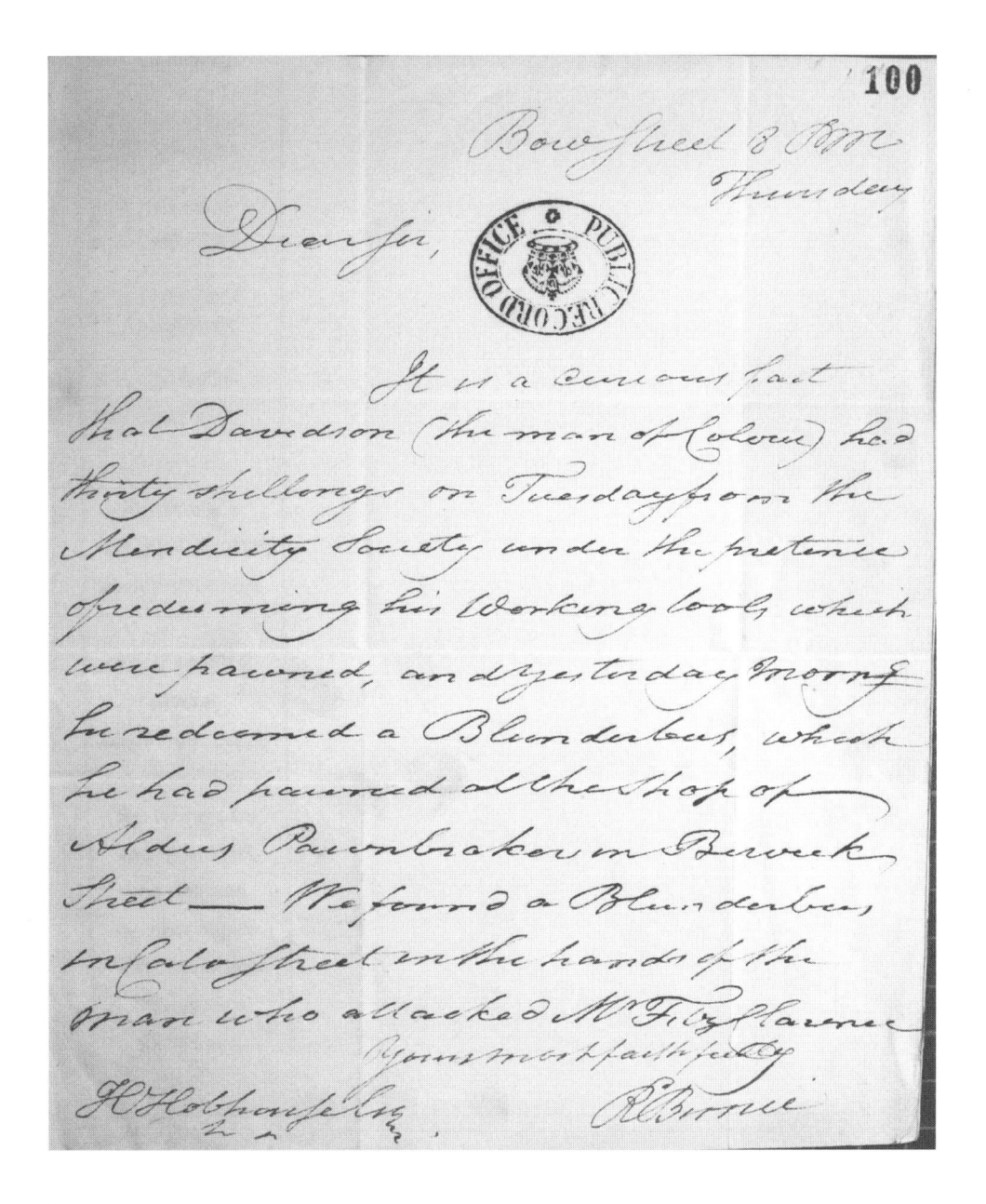

> **CONNECTION TO THE CURRICULUM**
> Ideas, political power, industry and empire: Britain, 1745–1901
> **Aim:** To find out about the role of William Davidson in the Cato Street Conspiracy.
> **Historical figure:** William Davidson (c. 1781–1820)
> **Source:** Letter by Richard Birnie to Henry Hobhouse (HO 44/4/100)

📖 TEACHER'S NOTES

What is this source?

This is a letter written by Richard Birnie to Henry Hobhouse. Birnie was the police magistrate at Bow Street in charge of the police officers who helped apprehend the Cato Street conspirators. Hobhouse was the permanent Under-Secretary of State 1817–27 at the Home Office.

What can we infer from this source?

This letter is handwritten and makes reference to a place, Bow Street, at '8pm on Thursday'. Bow Street has links to police history and was the site of London's first professional police force, which suggests that this letter is concerning a potential crime or incident of interest to the police. The author is writing about a man called Davidson, whom he describes as a 'man of colour'. He seems incredibly suspicious about Davidson's actions and behaviour, and explains that Davidson was given 30 shillings by the Mendicity Society to claim back his tools from the pawnbrokers. However, the author has discovered that Davidson did not redeem his tools at all. Instead he writes that Davidson used the money for a 'Blunderbuss' – a type of gun. We can also infer why this is of interest to the author, as it seems as though an incident or crime has occurred in Cato Street, where a man called Mr Fitzclarence was attacked. His attacker was discovered holding a Blunderbuss gun.

Why does The National Archives have this source?

This letter comes from records belonging to the Home Office (responsible for security, law and order). It is part of a much bigger file about the events of Cato Street in 1820.

What is the context of this source?

In February 1820, there was a plot to murder the British Cabinet Ministers and the Prime Minister Lord Liverpool. This became known as the Cato Street Conspiracy. The conspirators had fallen into a police trap as a government informer, George Edwards, had managed to infiltrate the group (and arguably helped to incite and inform their plans). The Mendicity Society was founded in 1818 to stop people begging in London. It gave help to beggars on the condition that they immediately left the area. Davidson deceived the society by asking for money to redeem his work tools, which he had pawned, and instead used the money to redeem a Blunderbuss.

Davidson was born in Jamaica. He was the illegitimate son of the Attorney General of Jamaica and a local woman. He travelled to Glasgow to study law and, whilst in Scotland, became involved in the movement for parliamentary reform. Press-ganged into the Royal Navy, Davidson moved to Birmingham following his discharge and resumed his interest in radical politics. He became a Spencean and helped to run the organisation. Davidson was one of the conspirators who was captured and tried for the Cato Street Conspiracy in 1820. During the trial, he protested his innocence:

'. . . you may suppose that because I am a man of colour I am without any understanding or feeling and would act the brute; I am not one of that sort; when not employed in my business, I have employed myself as a teacher of a Sunday-School...' (Howell's State Trials, vol. 33, cols. 1549–51 (1826))

Davidson was charged with high treason and hanged on 1st May 1820.

💡 LESSON IDEAS

ENQUIRY QUESTION
What does this document reveal about the role of William Davidson in the Cato Street Conspiracy?

Getting started

Use this letter to introduce the events of the Cato Street Conspiracy, the part played by Edwards and the role of William Davidson, in particular the way in which he felt he'd been judged unfairly because of his heritage. Many of the witnesses at the trial gave evidence about a 'man of colour' being involved, but did not directly identify Davidson as the person concerned.

Begin by introducing the students to the Cato Street Conspiracy. What happened? When was it? Who was involved and why?

Next introduce the source and ask students to try to read the original to begin with. Then, if required, hand out copies of the transcript available on page 52. Use questioning to ensure the students understand the meaning of the letter, explaining the terms 'Mendicity Society', 'blunderbuss' and 'pawnbrokers'.

Finally, tell the students more about William Davidson, his life and his involvement in the Cato Street Conspiracy.

Exploring further

Return to the source and use it to facilitate a class discussion to respond to the enquiry question: What does this document reveal about the role of William Davidson in the Cato Street Conspiracy?

Suggested prompt questions include:

- Can you make any inferences from the letter about why Davidson might have been involved in the Cato Street Conspiracy?
- Why do you think that Davidson had pawned his work tools?
- What impression has the author created about Davidson's character?
- What other sources would help us to find out about Davidson, Edwards and the other conspirators?

Round off the discussion by encouraging students to draw conclusions about the following:

- What is the significance of this attack in Cato Street and who is Mr Fitzclarence?
- What is Davidson's role in the incident and why is he important?

The students can then use the information drawn out during the discussion and their conclusions to write a short newspaper article reporting on the Cato Street Conspiracy and Davidson's role.

Follow-up tasks
- Ask students to create a storyboard of events leading up to the discovery of the Cato Street Conspiracy.

LESSON 11
William Davidson

TRANSCRIPT

Bow Street, 8pm
Thursday

Dear Sir,

It is a curious fact that Davidson (the man of colour) had thirty shillings on Tuesday from the Mendicity Society under the pretence of redeeming his working tools which were pawned, and yesterday morning he redeemed a Blunderbuss, which he had pawned at the shop of Alders Pawnbrokers on Berwick Street. We found a Blunderbuss in Cato Street in the hands of the man who attacked Mr Fitzclarence.

Yours most faithfully,

Richard Birnie
H. Hobhouse Esq

LESSON 12

THE JAMAICAN SLAVE REBELLION

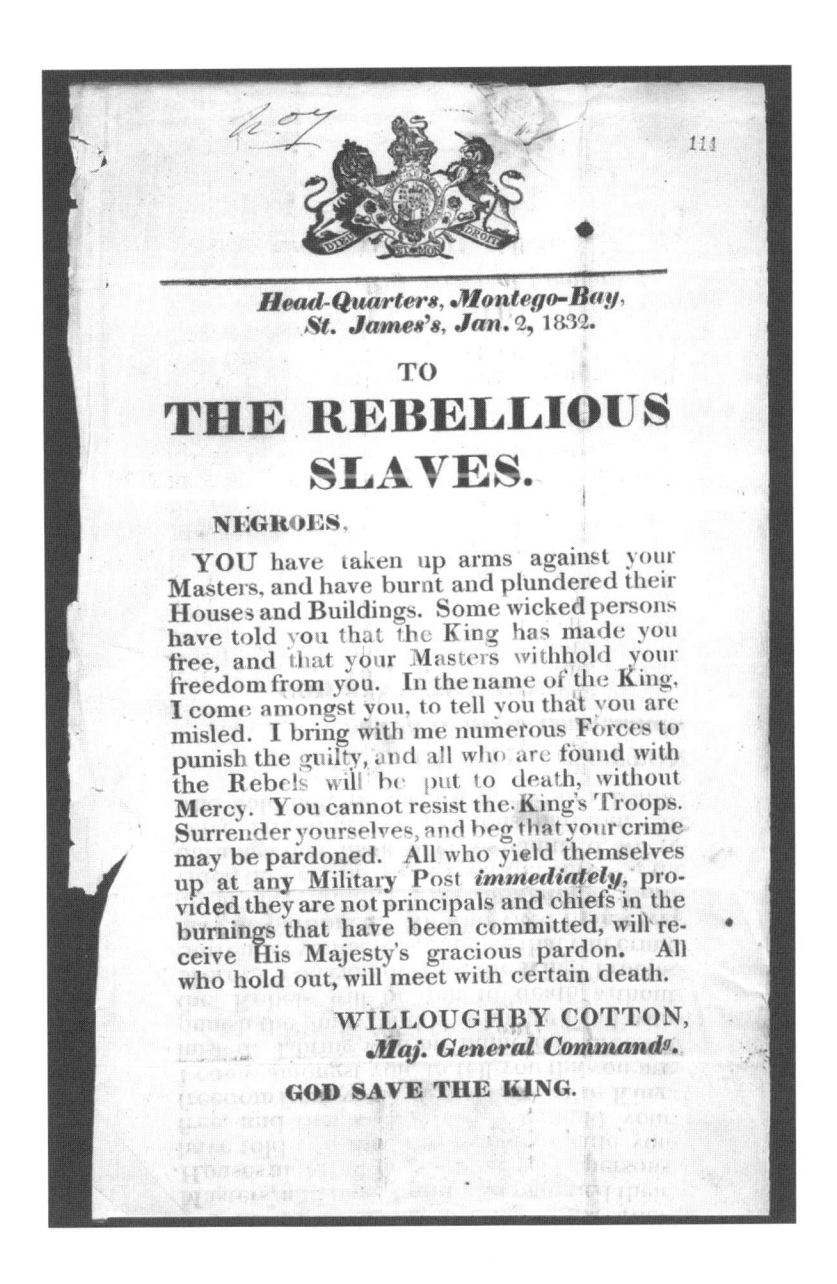

> **Head-Quarters, Montego-Bay,**
> **St. James's, Jan. 2, 1832.**
>
> **TO**
> **THE REBELLIOUS SLAVES.**
>
> **NEGROES,**
>
> YOU have taken up arms against your Masters, and have burnt and plundered their Houses and Buildings. Some wicked persons have told you that the King has made you free, and that your Masters withhold your freedom from you. In the name of the King, I come amongst you, to tell you that you are misled. I bring with me numerous Forces to punish the guilty, and all who are found with the Rebels will be put to death, without Mercy. You cannot resist the King's Troops. Surrender yourselves, and beg that your crime may be pardoned. All who yield themselves up at any Military Post *immediately*, provided they are not principals and chiefs in the burnings that have been committed, will receive His Majesty's gracious pardon. All who hold out, will meet with certain death.
>
> **WILLOUGHBY COTTON,**
> *Maj. General Commandᵍ.*
>
> **GOD SAVE THE KING.**

> **CONNECTION TO THE CURRICULUM**
>
> Ideas, political power, industry and empire: Britain, 1745–1901
>
> **Aim:** To find out about the Jamaican slave rebellion of 1831–32.
>
> **Historical event:** Jamaican slave rebellion
>
> **Source:** Poster addressed 'To the Rebellious Slaves' (CO 137/181 (114))
>
> **Caution:** This source contains language that is inappropriate and unacceptable today.

TEACHER'S NOTES

What is this source?

This is a poster that has come from a Colonial Office file. It is dated 1832 when Jamaica was under British colonial rule.

What can we infer from this source?

This poster has been produced on a printing press and the Royal Coat of Arms is displayed, suggesting it has been issued under the instructions of King William IV. The place of issue is listed as the 'Head-Quarters, Montego Bay', and the author is 'Willoughby Cotton', the 'Major General'. This reveals that it has been written in Jamaica and authorised by a senior military figure.

It is addressed directly to 'The Rebellious Slaves' using the pronoun 'you' throughout the text. Willoughby Cotton is writing in the first person, and this places the audience and the writer on opposing sides, with Willoughby depicted as the force of law and rightfulness.

In contrast, the enslaved people are described as 'rebellious' because they have 'taken up arms' against their masters. Willoughby emphasises the power of the 'King's Troops', threatening those who are rebelling with the punishment of death unless they surrender themselves. In contrast to this, the King himself is depicted as kind and gracious, offering a pardon to those who are not ringleaders and have not destroyed property. This is a stark choice – surrender or die.

The force and threat of this message reveal how concerned the authorities must have been about this rebellion. It poses a real threat to the order imposed by the British in Jamaica.

Why does The National Archives have this source?

This document is held within a Colonial Office File; it is from correspondence between the government and King in Britain, and the Governor General in Jamaica.

What is the context of this source?

Samuel Sharpe, a Black Baptist preacher on the island of Jamaica, instigated a peaceful 'general strike' against slavery in December 1831. He encouraged the enslaved people to refuse to return to work after their Christmas break until the slave owners listened to their demands for more freedom and a wage 'half the going wage-rate'. This strike coincided with the sugar-cane harvest, which Sharpe hoped would encourage plantation owners to listen to the enslaved people's demands.

Thomas Burchell, a missionary, returned to Jamaica from England after Christmas day. The Baptist ministry hoped that King William IV would have issued papers of emancipation for the enslaved and sent these back with Burchell. This was not the case.

On 27th December, some of the enslaved set fire to the Kensington Estate Great House. This fire was the beginning of escalating violence. Up to 60,000 enslaved people, out of the 300,000 who were enslaved in Jamaica, were involved in the rebellion over 11 days. Afterwards, many enslaved people were convicted and some were executed, including Samuel Sharpe. In 1975, Sharpe was posthumously made a National Hero by the Jamaican authorities for his resistance. Two years later, in 1834, slavery was abolished. It is argued that this rebellion was a significant moment on the journey to abolition.

💡 LESSON IDEAS

ENQUIRY QUESTION
What does this poster reveal about events on the island of Jamaica in late 1831 to 1832?

Getting started

Use this document to introduce the Jamaican Slave Rebellion.

Assuming your students already have knowledge of the slave trade, you could introduce the poster as a mystery document. Without giving any further information at this stage, ask students to look at the poster and then read through the text.

- Can students work out who has produced this poster and who the intended audience is?
- What does the document reveal about recent events in Jamaica at this time?

Accept all possible answers then explain the Jamaican Slave Rebellion, the context in which it took place and how events unfolded.

Exploring further

Now the students know more about the Jamaican Slave Rebellion, encourage them to revisit the poster and consider the text in more detail. In groups, ask them to discuss the following questions:

- What type of language is used to describe the enslaved people who have been rebelling?
- What does this reveal about the author's interpretation of their actions?
- Why will only some of the enslaved people involved be offered a pardon by the King?
- How is the King portrayed in this document?

Invite the students to share their findings with the rest of the class.

Finally, tell the students that two years after the rebellion, slavery was abolished.

As an extension to the lesson, explore what happened in Jamaica immediately after abolition in 1834. Most work available to former enslaved people was as 'apprentices'; lowly paid labour on the very same plantations and estates. James Williams was one such apprentice. You could offer students extracts from his account, published in *Facts and Documents Connected with the Late Insurrection in Jamaica: With a Narrative of Events Since the First Of August, 1834*, to support this part of the lesson. There are suitable extracts from the very first page of the narrative and Williams argued that 'apprenticeship' in fact worsened the conditions of former slaves who were treated harshly and unjustly incarcerated. The book is available for free on Google Books: **www.google.co.uk/books/edition/A_Narrative_of_Events_Since_the_First_of/7W1jAAAAcAAJ**

Follow-up tasks

- Students could investigate the life of Samuel Sharpe and some of his comrades, for example John Tharp or George Taylor, and prepare mini fact files on these individuals.
- Introduce students to the fictional story *Daddy Sharpe* by Fred W. Kennedy, which is written in the first person as Samuel Sharpe.
- Introduce students to *The Long Song* by Angela Levy, set against the backdrop of the Jamaican Rebellion of 1831–32.

LESSON 13

WILLIAM CUFFEY

> *William Cuffy Not Guilty – I demand a fair trial by a Jury of my peers and equals in accordance with Magna Charta*

> **CONNECTION TO THE CURRICULUM**
>
> Ideas, political power, industry and empire: Britain, 1745–1901
>
> **Aim:** To find out about the role of William Cuffey in the Chartist Movement.
>
> **Historical figure:** William Cuffey (also written Cuffay or Cuffy; 1788–1870)
>
> **Source:** Extract from papers for the trial of William Cuffey, William Lacey and Thomas Fay (TS 36/43)

📖 TEACHER'S NOTES

What is this source?

This document comes from the Treasury Solicitor's papers for the trial of William Cuffey.

What can we infer from this source?

This is part of a document that lists a number of men's names. Next to each of the men's names is the phrase 'Not Guilty', which suggests that this is a legal document relating to a criminal offence. We can infer that this is the plea of William Cuffey and not the trial's final verdict, as beside his name there is a further entry. It says, 'I demand a fair trial by a jury of my peers and equals in accordance with Magna Carta'.

The trial has not yet taken place, but Cuffey has concerns about the jury and the fact that they will all have to own property. This excluded many of Cuffey's peers – the working classes – from taking part in a jury. Cuffey is aware of this fact and is not afraid to say that this places him at a disadvantage.

Why does The National Archives have this source?

This record comes from the Treasury Solicitor's papers, acting on behalf of the Treasury and other government departments in legal matters.

What is the context of this source?

William Cuffey was the son of a former slave from St Kitt's, who had become a free man and married an English woman from Kent. Cuffey grew up in Chatham and became a journey-man tailor, serving his apprenticeship and learning his craft.

In 1834, along with other tailors, Cuffey went on strike from August to March to demand an eight-hour working day. The strike collapsed and Cuffey was 'black-listed', meaning he was denied work. Outraged at this treatment, Cuffey came to believe that the only way to achieve fair rights for workers was for them to be represented in Parliament. He began to play a prominent role in the Chartist Movement in London and in 1842 was elected to the national executive of the National Charter Association. By 1848, Cuffey had become so active within the movement that *The Times* newspaper referred to his section of Chartists as 'the Black man and his party'.

1848 was also the year of the Kennington Common Chartist demonstration. Cuffey and other leading Chartists were involved in organising the event, with around 25,000 people gathering together to prepare to march to Parliament with their petition for the 'People's Charter'. The government were concerned, fearing a non-peaceful meeting, so deployed additional special constables and other security measures. The march passed off peacefully and Feargus O'Connor and the Chartist Executive presented the petition to Parliament. It was rejected and the demonstration was declared a failure.

Shortly afterwards, Cuffey was arrested for conspiring to 'levy war against the Queen'. A government spy by the name of Powell had accused Cuffey and others of planning an armed uprising. Cuffey declared his innocence. The jury found him guilty and he was sentenced to transportation to Australia.

Cuffey was pardoned in 1856 but did not return to Britain. He chose to stay in Australia to continue the fight for political reform.

Diverse Histories © Clare Horrie and Rachel Hillman, 2022

💡 LESSON IDEAS

ENQUIRY QUESTION
What does this document reveal about William Cuffey and his role in the Chartist Movement?

Getting started

Use this document to introduce students to William Cuffey and how he was prominent within the Chartist Movement.

Firstly, ask the students to see if they can decipher any of the nineteenth-century handwriting. Can they make out any of the words? What do they think the document is about at this stage? Once they have had a go at reading the document, you can offer them a copy of the transcript if needed.

When the students have had time to look through the original image and transcript, ask them to consider the following:

- What type of document is this? What has led you to this conclusion?
- Who is Cuffey and what does the document reveal about his character?
- What other sources could we use to find out more about Chartism and Cuffey's role in the movement?

Exploring further

After the students have drawn their conclusions in the starter activity, use the teacher's notes to tell them more about the Chartist Movement and the role of William Cuffey.

We hear from Cuffey in a detailed trial report available on The National Archives website:
www.nationalarchives.gov.uk/pathways/blackhistory/rights/docs/cuffey_trial.htm

The words that Cuffey spoke in his defence at the trial are transcribed on the second and third pages. Ask the students to read this extract. What more can they find out about Cuffey in this document? How does this compare with the conclusions they drew from the original source document?

Finally, individually or in pairs, can the students now create a storyboard of the main events of Cuffey's life, reflecting his prominent role in the fight for political reform?

Follow-up tasks

- The students could use the documents and information gathered as the basis to write an obituary for William Cuffey.

LESSON 13
William Cuffey

TRANSCRIPT

| William Cuffy | Not Guilty – I demand a fair trial by a jury of my peers and equals in accordance with Magna Carta |

LESSON 14

MARY SEACOLE

CONNECTION TO THE CURRICULUM

Ideas, political power, industry and empire: Britain, 1745–1901

Aim: To find out about the significance of Mary Seacole in the Crimean War.

Historical figure: Mary Seacole (c. 1805–1881)

Source: Oil painting of Mary Seacole by Albert Charles Challen, 1869. National Portrait Gallery (item number: 6856) © National Portrait Gallery, London

TEACHER'S NOTES

What is this source?
This is an oil painting of Mary Seacole by London artist Albert Charles Challen (1847–81), created in 1869. It is on display at the National Portrait Gallery in London.

What can we infer from this source?
The portrait shows the head and shoulders of Mary Seacole. She appears as a middle-aged woman with touches of grey hair. Her face is lined and shown in profile looking to the left. She looks strong and characterful as though she has led a life of hard work. She is wearing a short red scarf around her neck and three medals, which she was awarded for her outstanding service in the Crimea. The medals are the British Crimean medal, the Turkish Order of the *Medjidie* and the French Legion of Honour. Why was this painting made? Possibly because by 1869, Mary Seacole was living in England, had published her autobiography and had been honoured by the medals shown in the painting. Perhaps it was commissioned to record her service, but it was lost to the nation until it was rediscovered in 2002.

Why does the National Portrait Gallery have it?
The painting was purchased with help from the National Lottery Heritage Fund and Gallery supporters in 2008. It is part of the National Portrait Gallery's main collection.

What is the context of this source?
This is the only known oil painting of Mary Seacole and it was discovered in 2002. The painting itself was actually hidden in the back of another framed print. It was sold at auction and bought by historian Helen Rappaport, an expert on Mary Seacole. The painting was later acquired by the National Portrait Gallery.

Mary Seacole worked tirelessly during the Crimean War (1853–56), nursing and caring for soldiers injured on the battlefields. Until the 1970s, historians exclusively focused on the contribution of her contemporary Florence Nightingale.

Seacole was born in Jamaica and was of mixed race. She left Jamaica in 1854 to apply to the War Office in England to work as an army nurse with Nightingale's nurses during the Crimean war. She was rejected, probably out of sheer prejudice and despite her earlier experience of nursing in a boarding house for invalids with her mother. Undaunted, she paid for her travel to the Crimea and set up the 'British Hotel' with Thomas Day near Balaclava for sick and injured soldiers to convalesce. She also showed great determination and courage to work as a female nurse in this male-dominated environment.

She returned to England in 1856 and published her autobiography, *Wonderful Adventures of Mrs Seacole in Many Lands*, in 1857, which was very popular. Mary Seacole died in Paddington, London, where she lived, and is buried in Kensal Green cemetery.

For more information about Mary Seacole, consult *Mary Seacole: The Most Famous Black Woman of the Victorian Age* by Jane Robinson, published 2004.

LESSON IDEAS

ENQUIRY QUESTION
What does this portrait reveal about the importance of Mary Seacole in the history of the Crimean War?

Getting started

Use this portrait to introduce the role of Mary Seacole in the history of army hospitals and how lessons were learned to lower the death rate among the wounded. Seacole is an important figure to study in parallel with her contemporary Florence Nightingale in the Crimea. Seacole and Nightingale highlight the difficulties for women working as nurses, but Seacole faced further difficulties because of her heritage.

In order to encourage your students to develop their observational skills for the interpretation of this source, introduce it using the 'five-second rule'. Give the class just five seconds to look at it on a whiteboard or printout. Ask them to remember anything they notice. Repeat a second time, but give them ten seconds to view it. What else have they noticed?

Exploring further

Now reveal the image for five to ten minutes and ask the students to jot down all the points they can make about the source. Suggested prompt questions to support your students in their observations include:

- Can you describe Mary Seacole's facial expression in the painting?
- What is she wearing?
- What can you infer from the medals?
- What impression has the artist created of her character?
- What are the advantages and disadvantages of using paintings as evidence for historians?

Now invite the students to share their responses in discussion with the aim of answering the enquiry question: what does this portrait reveal about the importance of Mary Seacole in the history of the Crimean War?

End the lesson with a written task. Ask the students to draw together all that has been discussed in order to write a newspaper article on the significance of Mary Seacole for nursing in the history of the Crimean War.

Follow-up tasks

- Look online to find a photograph of Mary Seacole's statue, which was unveiled at St Thomas's Hospital in 2016. Discuss in pairs how she is portrayed and how this compares to the oil painting. Why do you think it has taken a long time to create a statue in her memory? Are statues important for commemoration?
- Create two parallel timelines for the lives and achievements of Mary Seacole and Florence Nightingale. What are the similarities and differences between the lives and experiences of these two women?
- Read Mary Seacole's autobiography written in 1857 about her life, *Wonderful Adventures of Mrs Seacole in Many Lands*. How does it compare to the accounts of her life that we find in secondary school textbooks?

LESSON 15

THE JUBILEE SINGERS

THE JUBILEE SINGERS, from FISK UNIVERSITY, Nashville, Tennessee, U.S.A., will give TWO CONCERTS, at the QUEEN'S CONCERT ROOMS, Hanover-square, on MONDAY EVENING NEXT, MAY 12, commencing at Eight o'Clock, and on SATURDAY MORNING, MAY 17, commencing at Three o'Clock. Stalls (numbered and reserved), 5s.; Second Seats, 2s. 6d.; Admission, 1s. Tickets may be had of Mr. Hall, at the Hanover-square Rooms; Mr. Austin, St. James's Hall; Messrs. Chappell, 50, New Bond-street; Mr. Mitchell, 33, Old Bond-street; Messrs. Keith, Prowse, and Co., 48, Cheapside; and of Mr. Hays, 4, Royal Exchange-buildings, E.C.

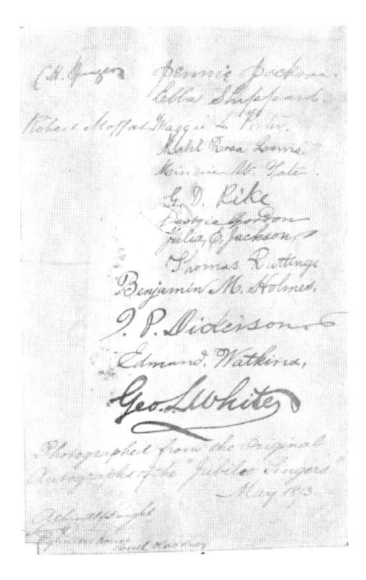

Men standing at the back from left to right: Edmund Watkins; I. P. Dickerson; Benjamin M. Holmes; Thomas Rutling.
Women seated from the left to right: Georgia Gordon; Mabel Rosa Lewis; Maggie L. Porter; Jennie Jackson [centre]; Ella Sheppard; Julia Jackson; Minniver U. Yates.

CONNECTION TO THE CURRICULUM

Ideas, political power, industry and empire: Britain, 1745–1901

Aim: To explore the diversity of musical culture in the 1870s.

Historical figures: The Jubilee Singers

Sources: Extract from the *Illustrated London News*, 10th May 1873 (ZPER 34/62); photograph of the Jubilee Singers (COPY 1/25 f182) and signatures of the Jubilee Singers

TEACHER'S NOTES

What is this source?

The first source is an extract from the *Illustrated London News*, 10th May 1873.

The second source is entitled 'Photograph of the Jubilee Singers from Fisk University, United States of America, four male figures standing and seven females sitting'.

A third source (filed with the photograph) shows signatures of the Jubilee Singers, dated May 1873.

What can we infer from these sources?

The extract from the *Illustrated London News* reveals that the Jubilee Singers performed in London in May 1873. This announcement marks the start of their tour in Britain. We learn about the date, time and price of tickets for the performance. We can infer from the source that it was a significant musical event.

From the photograph we can infer that this is from the mid-Victorian period according to their style of dress. The picture is clearly posed and not naturalistic in any way, owing to the type of camera technology at the time, and obviously is not in colour. The group look very smart as they are public performers. The women have their hair elaborately arranged and are wearing bows at their necks and the men are wearing bow ties.

The autograph 'list' document is interesting because it contains more names. It suggests the group was larger. It also includes George L. Cole, the musical director of the group and a White ex-soldier from the American Civil War. The purpose of the photograph was to show the main singers of the group.

Why does The National Archives have this source?

The photograph was registered for copyright on 22nd June 1874 and is held in the Copyright collection.

What is the context of these sources?

Fisk University, in Nashville Tennessee, was founded in 1866 by the American Missionary Association. The university aimed to educate freed African Americans after the abolition of slavery in 1865. The Jubilee Singers grew out of an early singing class held at the university aimed at fundraising for the college. Their name was a reference to the Year of Jubilee in *Leviticus 25* when the enslaved should be set free.

The nine Jubilee Singers were directed by George L. White, previously a soldier, and in 1871 they toured North America. The youngest member was 14-year-old Minniver Tate. From the start, their musical repertoire was wide ranging and included popular songs as well as classical compositions. They went on to incorporate slave songs and Black spiritual music, which audiences loved.

The Jubilee Singers toured in Britain. The notice in the *Illustrated London News* records their performances in London on the 12th and 17th May 1873. They also performed for Queen Victoria. The Queen's Concert Rooms were used for many different purposes apart from music and balls, including public meetings. Outside the capital, they went on to perform in Hull and Leeds in 1873. They toured the United Kingdom for a year and later travelled to Europe. They raised £10,000 for funding a new hall for their university.

Diverse Histories © Clare Horrie and Rachel Hillman, 2022

💡 LESSON IDEAS

ENQUIRY QUESTION
What does this source reveal about the music enjoyed by people in this period?

Getting started
Use these sources to introduce the Jubilee Singers. Explain to the students that their music was enjoyed in the later part of nineteenth century.

Exploring further
Ask the students to examine one of the three sources in a small group. Use the prompt questions below if needed. Ask students to feed back to the rest of the class on their source. Discuss what additional information photographs provide which written documents might not. Discuss which source is: most useful, interesting, surprising or accessible.

Explore other musical genres that were also popular at the time. Do we enjoy the same music today?

Newspaper article
1. What type of source is this?
2. Why do you think this article was written?
3. What impression does the article give of the singing group?
4. Can you explain your reasons?
5. How would you describe the tone of the article?
6. How can we date this article?
7. What does a written article reveal which a photograph might not?
8. What does this source reveal about the role of women?
9. What other sources would help us to find out more about the Jubilee Singers?

Photograph
- Why do you think this photograph was taken?
- What impression does the photograph give of the singing group?
- Can you describe the style of this photograph?
- How can we date this photograph?
- What does a photograph reveal which a written document might not?
- What does this source reveal about the role of women?
- What other sources would help us to find out more about the Jubilee Singers?

💡 LESSON IDEAS

Signatures

1. What type of source is this?
2. Why do you think this source was produced?
3. What impression does the source give of the singing group?
4. How can we date this source?
5. What does this source reveal about the role of women?
6. What other sources would help us to find out more about the Jubilee Singers?

Follow-up tasks

- Produce a tour advert for the Jubilee Singers visiting Britain from 1873 to 1874.
- Look at this illustrated website which describes their tour in Yorkshire: **www.africansinyorkshireproject.com/fisk-jubilee-singers-part-one.html**
- Listen to 'Swing Low Sweet Chariot' from the Jubilee Singers, which is available online. Write a review of their singing.

LESSON 15
The Jubilee Singers

TRANSCRIPT

C.H. Springer Robert Moffat	Jennie Jackson Ella Sheppard Maggie L. Porter Mabel Rosa Lewis Minniver U. Yates G. D. Rike Georgia Gordon Julia Jackson Thomas Rutling Benjamin M. Holmes I. P. Dickerson Edmund Watkins George L. White [Director]
Athro Alfred Knight, Eglington House, South Hackney	Photographed from the original autographs of the Jubilee Singers, May 1873

LESSON 16

SAMUEL COLERIDGE-TAYLOR

> **CONNECTION TO THE CURRICULUM**
> Ideas, political power, industry and empire: Britain, 1745–1901
> **Aim:** To broadly explore the diversity of musical culture in this period.
> **Historical figure:** Samuel Coleridge-Taylor (1875–1912)
> **Source:** Photograph of Samuel Coleridge-Taylor (COPY 1/483)

📖 TEACHER'S NOTES

What is this source?

This is a photograph which was registered in 1905 at Stationer's Hall under the copyright acts in force from 1842 to 1912. The title of the photograph is 'Samuel Coleridge-Taylor'. There was no other information about the subject or the photographer.

What can we infer from this source?

We can infer from the photograph that Samuel Coleridge-Taylor was a significant person. He appears well dressed and confident and he has presence. This is an example of a portrait-style photograph. He is seated in a carved wooden high-backed chair, which looks like something designed in the spirit of the Arts and Crafts movement started by William Morris in the 1860s. The movement aimed to improve the quality and accessibility of design. Fabric and furniture frequently employed plant forms and natural materials. Does this provide a possible link to the person in the photograph? Why was this photograph taken? Was it a publicity photograph for Samuel Coleridge-Taylor? Was it for a newspaper article or magazine? Did Coleridge-Taylor commission it?

Why does The National Archives have this source?

The photograph is one of two photographs from the COPY 1 copyright collection, which we can detect from the document reference. Photographers and artists would copyright their work by registering it at Stationer's Hall in London. This meant that they had control over how their images were used.

What is the context of this source?

Samuel Coleridge-Taylor was born in London in 1875 and died in 1912. He was a composer and conductor of mixed race. He was named after the poet Samuel Taylor Coleridge.

This photograph was dated in 1905 so it shows Samuel Coleridge-Taylor aged 32 years. He died tragically five years later from pneumonia.

Samuel Coleridge-Taylor married musician Jessie Walmisley in 1899; they had two children together who also went on to have musical careers.

In his compositions he combined African-American folk music with orchestral music, and was known in New York, problematically, as the 'African Mahler'. He went on tour in America in 1904, 1906 and 1910. He was highly successful in his short career; one of his most famous works, created between 1898 and 1900, is called *The Song of Hiawatha*. The composer Edward Elgar was a supporter of Coleridge-Taylor's great talent.

Diverse Histories © Clare Horrie and Rachel Hillman, 2022

LESSON IDEAS

ENQUIRY QUESTION
What does this source reveal about the music enjoyed by people in this period?

Getting started

Use this source to introduce the composer Samuel Coleridge-Taylor. His work is an example of the classical music that people enjoyed at the start of the twentieth century.

Share the source with the class and explain that this is a photograph of the famous musician Samuel Coleridge-Taylor. Don't give any further information at this point. Allow the class to brainstorm their own questions to discover what they can learn from the source and then discuss their answers as a group. Below are some suggestions:

- What type of source is this?
- Why was this photograph taken?
- What impression of Samuel Coleridge-Taylor does the photograph give?
- Can you explain your reasons?
- Can you describe the style of this photograph?
- How can we date this photograph?
- What does a photograph reveal which a written document might not?
- What other sources would help us to find out more about Samuel Coleridge-Taylor?

Exploring further

Now the class has studied the photograph, provide them with more information about Samuel Coleridge-Taylor using the teacher's notes. Tell the pupils about Coleridge-Taylor's heritage, his life, and his career as a composer. Now the pupils know more about his life and work, ask them to revisit the questions and answers they came up with in the starter task. How much of this information were they able to ascertain from the photograph? How many of their inferences were accurate? What more do they think the photograph can tell them now they know a little more about Coleridge-Taylor?

As a class, explore Coleridge-Taylor's musical works, listening to some excerpts using video clips on YouTube. Explain that Coleridge-Taylor combined African-American folk music with orchestral music. Why do the students think he might have chosen to do this? (A possible answer would be to celebrate African-American music and help introduce it to new audiences.)

Now listen to some of the 'Ragtime' music of American composer Scott Joplin (1868–1917) from roughly the same period. Compare and contrast this music with that of Coleridge-Taylor. What conclusions can be drawn from these sources about the music enjoyed by people in the late eighteenth and early nineteenth centuries?

Finally, students could explore other musical genres that were also popular at the time.

Follow-up tasks

- Use the internet to research further into Samuel Coleridge-Taylor's life. Create a timeline of significant events and a family tree.
- Produce a leaflet for tourists on the significance of Coleridge-Taylor, including images of the two blue plaques to be found for him in London.
- Use Google to relisten to one of Samuel Coleridge-Taylor's compositions and then write a review of this composition.

LESSON 17

ABDUL KARIM

the Queen at Work.

CONNECTION TO THE CURRICULUM
Ideas, political power, industry and empire: Britain, 1745–1901
Aim: To find out about the role of Abdul Karim in Queen Victoria's household.
Historical figure: Abdul Karim (1863–1909)
Source: Photograph of Abdul Karim and Queen Victoria (COPY 1/449 (334))

TEACHER'S NOTES

What is this source?

This photograph comes from a series of documents that were registered at Stationer's Hall in London under the Copyright Acts that existed from 1842 to 1912.

What can we infer from this source?

This photograph shows an image of Queen Victoria seated outside under an awning. The area looks like it has been prepared to make a comfortable working environment for the Queen, with a large rug and footstall underneath her desk and cushioned seating. This suggests that she has a number of hours' work to undertake in her 'outdoor study'. She is dressed quite warmly, with a hat and a heavy coat, so it is unlikely to be the height of summer!

On the desk are a number of boxes, possibly containing correspondence and paperwork that the Queen is attending to. She is focusing her attention on the document in front of her and appears to be writing. There are some further boxes of paperwork resting on an additional chair on the right-hand side.

To the left of the Queen's desk stands a man of Indian descent wearing a turban and traditional Indian clothing. He is holding a stick and is standing very straight, with his well-polished, gleaming shoes highlighted by the pale colour of the rug. He looks like he is watching over the Queen, or perhaps waiting to serve her should he be needed. The photograph suggests that he is not visiting or meeting with the Queen and is not of equal rank, as he isn't seated and the Queen's attention is intently focused on the work in front of her.

Why does The National Archives have this source?

This photograph comes from the COPY 1 copyright collection. People such as artists, designers, inventors and photographers would copyright their work by registering it at Stationer's Hall. This meant nobody could use their work without their permission.

What is the context of this source?

This photograph shows Abdul Karim. Karim arrived in Britain from India in 1887, following Queen Victoria's Golden Jubilee. In 1894, he was given the role of Queen Victoria's Indian Secretary, meaning he had the responsibility of helping the Queen with her 'boxes' and correspondence. 'Boxes' referred to the despatch boxes full of documents that the Queen received from parliament, government and her own private secretary.

Karim soon became highly valued and regarded by the Queen. His presence and proximity to her in the photograph reflects the important role that he played in her household. Queen Victoria also made Karim her native language teacher, known as a 'Munshi', and he taught her Hindustani. She bestowed numerous titles and land upon him, calling him her 'Indian John Brown'. Despite being so highly regarded by Queen Victoria, Karim wanted to return to India as he felt like 'a sojourner in a strange land among strange people' (quoted in *Victoria & Abdul* by Shrabani Basu). The Queen's favour also stirred up hostility within the court and royal family.

When Queen Victoria died in 1901, Karim returned to India. She left Karim a plot of land and money in her will, yet another reflection of the esteem that she had held him in.

💡 LESSON IDEAS

ENQUIRY QUESTION
What does this document reveal about Abdul Karim and his role in Queen Victoria's household?

Getting started

Use this document to introduce students to Abdul Karim and how he became a servant in Queen Victoria's household, before being promoted to Munshi and becoming a highly regarded confidante of the Queen.

Show the source photograph to the students and use questioning to draw out some of the observations and inferences explored in the teacher's notes:

- What can you see in the photograph?
- Who are these two people?
- What are they doing?
- What might their relationship be?

Using the teacher's notes on the previous page, provide some basic background information about Abdul Karim and his life in Queen Victoria's household.

Exploring further

Return to the photograph and ask the students to look at it again now they understand its context. Encourage the students to observe the photograph in more detail and discuss the following:

- Ask the students to describe Abdul Karim's dress and stance in the photograph. What can this reveal about his role, status and relationship with the Queen?
- Why do you think Queen Victoria had this photograph of Karim and her taken?

- What other sources could we use to find out more about Abdul Karim and his role in Queen Victoria's household?

Provide some further information about the life of Abdul Karim; students can then use this to create a presentation about Abdul Karim's life in Queen Victoria's household.

Before the end of the lesson, explain what happened to Abdul Karim once Queen Victoria had died. Discuss why Edward VII made him burn all of the letters and papers Karim had been given by Queen Victoria after her death.

Follow-up tasks
- Introduce students to Shrabani Basu's work, *Victoria & Abdul: The True Story of the Queen's Closest Confidant.*

LESSON 18

THE BRITISH EMPIRE IN THE VICTORIAN PERIOD

CONNECTION TO THE CURRICULUM

Ideas, political power, industry and empire: Britain, 1745–1901

Aim: To explore the rise of the British Empire in the Victorian period.

Historical figure: Imre Kiralfy

Source: Poster for Imre Kiralfy's Historical Production of India (COPY 1/118 f.230)

TEACHER'S NOTES

What is this source?

This poster was registered in 1895 at Stationer's Hall under the copyright acts in force from 1842 to 1912.

What can we infer from this source?

The poster was publicity for a historical spectacle held at Earl's Court, London in 1895 by the promoter Imre Kiralfy. We can see on the left a scene showing 'Sir Thomas Roe before the Great Moghul Jehanghir in 1616' and on the right another scene showing the 'Proclamation of the Queen as Empress of India in 1877'. The poster seems to be presenting a version of the history of India through the eyes of the British and a justification for the British Empire. It says more about Britain than India. The imagery arguably suggests a superior Britain, led by Queen Victoria as Empress, bringing a civilising influence to the government of this continent.

We can also infer from the poster that the production anticipates drawing in large crowds. Earl's Court was a large site. The development of extensive train and bus services by the 1890s could bring in visitors.

Finally, the poster suggests that Imre Kiralfy was a well-known impresario for this type of show and it is advertising the 1895 'season'. The advertisement would have been displayed in public spaces and the press. What does the performance suggest about entertainment at the time? What does it suggest about views of Empire in the period?

Why does The National Archives have this source?

The poster is from the COPY 1 copyright collection which we can detect from the document reference. Artists would copyright their work by registering it at Stationer's Hall in London. This meant that they had control over how their images were used.

What is the context of this source?

The Earl's Court Exhibition Grounds included the two-storey Empress Theatre, which could seat 6,000 viewers for Kiralfy's spectacle about the history of India, told through song, dance and mime. For further entertainment there was a large Ferris wheel, with the capacity for 1,200 people. The patrons of the exhibition included four Maharajas and four Rajas with various members of the British aristocracy. Props and artefacts were obtained from India for the numerous sets built by workers who were brought over from India.

Imre Kiralfy (1845–1919) and his younger brother Bolossy (1848–1932) were born in Budapest and were from a Hungarian Jewish background. They toured throughout Europe as dancers with their family. Later the brothers went into business together producing various shows in Europe and America but split up in 1887. Imre moved to England and became a British citizen. He is buried in Kensal Green Cemetery in London.

💡 LESSON IDEAS

ENQUIRY QUESTION
What does this source reveal about the British Empire?

Getting started

First *define* the term 'British Empire'. Explore how the source helps us to define it by thinking through the following questions as a class:

- What does the content of the spectacle reveal about perceptions of Empire?
- Does the source suggest the popularity of the Empire at the time?
- What does the source suggest about the role of Queen Victoria?

Share with the students a map showing the extent of the British Empire in 1895, the date of this source, examining it closely together.

Exploring further

The students prepare a report on the case for including this source in an exhibition about the British Empire. They can use the following questions to help structure their report:

- What type of source is this?
- Why do you think it was created?
- What is the content of this source?
- How can we date this source?
- What does the source reveal about leisure and entertainment in the 1890s?
- What does this source reveal about the British Empire?
- What other sources should be in the exhibition to provide further information and perspectives on the British Empire?

Follow-up tasks

- Create your own map to understand the extent of the British Empire by 1901 and an accompanying timeline to show the establishment of the British Empire.
- Write and deliver a presentation explaining when these countries were made part of the Empire.
- Make a list of all of the productions produced by the Kiralfy brothers (together and independently). Do they have common themes? Do any others relate to the British Empire?

PART 3

CHALLENGES FOR BRITAIN, EUROPE AND THE WIDER WORLD: 1901 TO THE PRESENT DAY

LESSON 19

SOPHIA DULEEP SINGH

Princess Sophia Dhuleep Singh selling "The Suffragette" outside Hampton Court Palace, where she has a suite of apartments.

CONNECTION TO THE CURRICULUM
Challenges for Britain, Europe and the wider world: 1901 to the present day

Aim: To find out about Sophia Duleep Singh and her role in the Suffragette movement.

Historical figure: Sophia Duleep Singh (1876–1948)

Source: Photograph of Sophia Duleep Singh (ASSI 52/212/17)

📖 TEACHER'S NOTES

What is this source?

This is a photograph within a newspaper cutting that comes from documents held in the records of Justices of Assizes (the assizes were periodic criminal courts held around England and Wales until 1972). The newspaper it comes from is *The Suffragette*, the official newspaper of the Women's Social and Political Union (WSPU) and first published in 1912. It included information about militant activities, as well as other information that might have appealed to its readership.

What can we infer from this source?

This cutting shows a photograph of a woman of Indian descent, well dressed in upper-class Victorian fashion. She is wearing a hat, her hair is neatly styled and her coat looks as if it is made from an expensive fabric. She is standing outside, possibly in some type of public garden or park, and it looks like she has positioned herself on a footpath where people might be passing. To the right in the photograph there is a large, moveable board that displays the words 'Suffragette Revolution!' (Perhaps the woman has brought this with her to display?). The woman is also wearing a large bag across her shoulders, which appears to be full of newspapers. She is holding one of these newspapers in her hand, so that the front page and title are visible to people walking past. It reads *The Suffragette*.

At the bottom of the photograph there is a caption, which suggests that this image has been clipped out of a bigger page in a newspaper. It says 'Sophia Dhuleep Singh selling "The Suffragette" outside Hampton Court Palace where she has a suite of apartments'. The newspaper has used a different spelling for the family name, although Duleep was the preferred spelling.

Why does The National Archives have this source?

This image is held within an assizes file. These files relate to records of criminal courts that were held around England and Wales until 1972. This is possibly being used as evidence in a criminal case, perhaps as an example of material designed to 'incite' people to join the Women's Social and Political Union. The very existence of this newspaper in a government file of this nature implies that it was not a publication that the government condoned and approved of.

What is the context of this source?

This photograph shows a princess named Sophia Alexandrovna Duleep Singh. Her father was the Maharaja Sir Duleep Singh, who at ten years old had been deposed from the Punjab and exiled to England. Sophia joined the WSPU in 1909 and became a prominent suffragette and campaigner for women's rights. Her position as the deposed Maharaja's daughter, and as the goddaughter of Queen Victoria, meant that she could champion the cause of women's suffrage in a way that attracted public interest.

Sophia participated in the Black Friday events of November 1910 and other suffragette activities. She also regularly sold copies of *The Suffragette* newspaper outside Hampton Court, where she lived in a 'grace and favour' apartment. Along with the fight for female suffrage, Sophia also campaigned for Indian independence and the care of Indian soldiers during the First World War.

💡 LESSON IDEAS

ENQUIRY QUESTION
What does this document reveal about Princess Sophia Duleep Singh and her role in the Suffragette movement?

Getting started

Use this document to introduce students to Sophia Duleep Singh and her role in the Women's Social and Political Union (WSPU).

Display the source on the whiteboard or hand out a printout. Without giving any information yet, ask students to make observations about the photograph and draw inferences from these observations. Where do they think this source might have come from? What does it show? Who is Sophia Duleep Singh?

Accept the students' answers before going on to explain that the woman in the photograph is Sophia Duleep Singh and she had an important role in the suffragette movement. At this point, use questioning to ensure the students have a solid understanding of the aims of the suffragette movement. You might need to provide some further information and context.

Exploring further

Take another look at the photograph with the students to see if they can use it to find out anything more about Sophia Duleep Singh.

Firstly, ask the students to describe Sophia Duleep Singh's dress and stance in the photograph. What can this reveal about her status in society? Once the students have considered this independently, tell them that Sophia Duleep Singh was an Indian princess and explain more about her background and status, using the teacher's notes. How might Sophia Duleep Singh's status in society have benefited her campaigning?

Now look at the photograph again and discuss the following questions:

- Why do you think Sophia Duleep Singh chose to sell *The Suffragette* outside Hampton Court Palace in this way?
- Do you think she knowingly posed for this photograph? Why/why not?
- What other sources could we use to find out more about Sophia Duleep Singh, her role in the suffragette movement and also her support for other important causes?

Make it clear to the students that Sophia Duleep Singh campaigned for other causes in addition to women's suffrage, including Indian independence and the care of Indian soldiers in the First World War.

Follow-up tasks

- Ask the students to imagine they are going to interview someone with expert knowledge of Sophia Duleep Singh for a podcast. What questions would they ask to find out more about Sophia Duleep Singh's role in the suffragette movement and her support for other causes? Can they find out the answers to these questions for homework?
- Introduce students to Anita Anand's work, *Sophia: Princess, Suffragette, Revolutionary*.
- Discuss in pairs or as a class why you think Sophia Duleep Singh was such a prominent figure within the suffragette movement.

LESSON 20

WALTER TULL

> **CONNECTION TO THE CURRICULUM**
> First World War 1914–1918 and Peace Settlement
> **Aim:** To recognise the contribution of Black service men in the First Word War.
> **Historical figure:** Walter Tull (1888–1918)
> **Source:** War Office record for Walter Tull (WO 339/90293)

TEACHER'S NOTES

What is this source?
This is a document from the War Office about Walter Tull.

What can we infer from this source?
At the start of the First World War, Walter Tull joined the army in the 17th (1st Football) Battalion of the Middlesex Regiment as a Lance-Corporal. He was later made an officer, a leader of men, as this document suggests. The document is his application for a 'temporary commission' as an officer.

As the First World War continued, more men were needed to fight, especially after the huge losses at the Battle of the Somme, and more men were needed as commanding officers. This meant that men from a wider variety of ethnic and social backgrounds could, potentially for the first time, become officers, as the army was forced to abandon its rules concerning race. It is important to note that Black service men had served in the British Army and Navy before the First World War but had never been allowed to become officers.

Walter Tull's application was successful. He was promoted to Second Lieutenant after officer training school at Gailes, Scotland. He became the first Afro-Caribbean mixed-heritage soldier to be commissioned as an infantry officer in the British Army.

Why does The National Archives have this source?
The document comes from the War Office collections, which we can detect from the document reference beginning in WO.

What is the context of this source?
Tull's father's father had been enslaved on a plantation in Barbados. Before the war, Walter Tull was a professional footballer. He played in the First Division of the Football League for Tottenham Hotspur in 1909 and later for Northampton Town FC in 1911. Walter Tull was one of the first Black professional players in the football league in this country, and this was significant in starting to make the sport more inclusive. He was a very good player, but he received racial abuse from some of the people watching the football matches at the time.

He joined the Army in December 1914, serving in the Middlesex Regiment, including its two Football Battalions. He was later made a sergeant and served in France in 1915. He returned briefly to recover from shellshock, or what we would now call post-traumatic stress disorder. He returned to fight in the Battle of the Somme and then came home to recover from trench fever. After his recovery, he went on to officer training where he was commissioned. He joined the 23rd Battalion, Middlesex Regiment (the 2nd Footballers) in August 1917. The battalion served in the Third Battle of Ypres and then Italy in November 1917. Tull was thus significantly a Black officer and leader of White troops into battle. The following year, he was recommended for the Military Cross but this was not granted.

His battalion returned to France to take part in the Spring Offensive on 23rd March 1918. Tull died aged 29 during a heavy bombardment near the Arras-Bapaume Road. There are nearly 35,000 casualties listed, including Walter Tull, on the Arras Memorial for the Missing in the Cemetery at Faubourg d'Amiens.

💡 LESSON IDEAS

ENQUIRY QUESTION

What does this document reveal about the importance of Walter Tull in the history of the First World War?

Getting started

Start by defining the key words in the document:

- temporary commission
- battalion
- regiment
- sergeant.

Now ask the students to read the document and take it in turns, in pairs, to ask and answer the following questions:

- What type of source is this?
- What was Tull's full name?
- When was he born?
- Was he married?
- What can you find out about Tull's career in the army from this document?
- Can you find out where he saw action in the First World War?
- What other sources could be used to show the significance of Walter Tull in history?

Exploring further

Come back together as a class and discuss the key facts that can be ascertained from the document, before going on to share any further details from the teacher's notes on the previous page.

Using all the information that has been gathered during the lesson so far, the students can write a newspaper article on the significance of Walter Tull in the history of the First World War.

Follow-up tasks

- This lesson can be followed by Lesson 23 on Euan Lucie-Smith, an officer of mixed British and Afro-Caribbean heritage, in order to further explore the contributions of Black servicemen in the First World War.
- Investigate Walter Tull's sporting career further. Create an illustrated leaflet explaining his significance in the history of sport with regards to his football career. Include the teams he played for at home and abroad before the war.
- Teachers consult *Black British History: New Perspectives*, edited by Hakim Adi. Provide students with some extracts from Chapter 3 on the commemoration of African and Caribbean Servicemen to read in class or as homework. The class can then discuss the idea of commemoration after the First World War. How were Black British and Colonial servicemen commemorated after the war?

LESSON 21

NAIK DARWAN SING NEGI

> wounded. There were, of course, many instances of distinguished courage and devotion which will never be recorded. One however has won for an Indian soldier the Victoria Cross. First in every dash on the traverses with the bayonet, three times wounded, Naik Darwan Sing Negi of the i/39th Garhwal Rifles did not even report his wounds till his company fell in.
>
> Such is the story of an action which is dwarfed by the magnitude of the struggle in which we are engaged. It will add nevertheless one more page to the glorious history of Briton and Indian side by side in arms.
>
> Sd. R.A. Steel.
> Major.
>
> Indian Corps Headquarters.
> December 12th, 1914.

CONNECTION TO THE CURRICULUM
Challenges for Britain, Europe and the wider world: 1901 to the present day
Aim: To recognise the contribution of Indian servicemen in the First World War.
Historical figure: Naik Darwan Sing Negi (dates unknown)
Source: Extract from the War Diary of the 57th Wilde's Rifles, 1914–15 (WO 95/3923/002)

📖 TEACHER'S NOTES

What is this source?

This is an extract taken from the War Diary of the 57th Wilde's Rifles. Unit War Diaries like this are kept within files belonging to the War Office, giving a record of operations. The War Diary was the responsibility of the commander of every military unit, and was compiled for each month that the unit was on active service.

What can we infer from this source?

This extract from the War Diary of the 57th Wilde's Rifles (1st August 1914 to 31st December 1915) has been typewritten. It refers to 'many instances of distinguished courage' on the frontline that will 'never be recorded'. However, it does make reference to a soldier named Naik Darwan Sing Negi, who has been awarded the Victoria Cross.

We know that Sing Negi was an Indian soldier as the diary refers to his nationality. He has been awarded the Victoria Cross, so must have behaved with significant courage on the battlefield. The author of the War Diary holds Sing Negi in high regard and has been impressed by his actions. He describes how Sing Negi was 'three times injured' by the bayonet and how he 'did not even report his wounds until his company fell in'.

The extract acknowledges the fact that many courageous soldiers' actions will go unmentioned and in the final paragraph 'the magnitude of the struggle in which we are engaged'. The writer adds that these actions will add 'to the glorious history of Briton and Indian side by side in arms'. This narrative of loyalty and unity implies a harmonious relationship and provides no information about the pockets of dissent that did exist amongst some Indian recruits.

Why does The National Archives have this source?

This document is an extract from a War Diary held within a War Office file. The War Office was a department of the British government that was in charge of the army.

What is the context of this source?

During the First World War, around 138,600 Indian soldiers fought on the Western Front in support of Britain. The 57th Wilde's Rifles fought alongside British soldiers, trying to recover trenches lost near Festubert on 23rd and 24th November 1914.

Indian soldiers were key contributors to the Allied forces and suffered many casualties. They were praised for their courage, and out of 11 Victoria Crosses awarded during the conflict, eight were given to Indian soldiers.

Although many soldiers took pride in fighting for Britain, there were pockets of dissent and discontent. Some felt that Indian soldiers were sent into the trenches ahead of White soldiers to take the most aggressive fire. Yet there was never a movement of widespread discontent. By the end of the war, almost 1.5 million Indians had volunteered for the Indian Expeditionary Force; 50,000 of these men were killed, another 65,000 injured and over 10,000 were declared missing.

It's important to note that historical discussions about the 'Indian contribution' to the war refer to 'British India' from 1858 to 1947, which comprises present-day India, Pakistan, Bangladesh and Burma.

💡 LESSON IDEAS

ENQUIRY QUESTION
Use this document to introduce students to the significant contribution that India made to support Britain during the First World War.

Getting started

Ask the students to read the extract and discuss the following questions in groups:

- What does this document reveal about Naik Darwan Sing Negi and his actions?
- What emotion does the writer express about Sing Negi?
- Why do you think he feels this way?

Now come together as a class to discuss the students' responses and draw some conclusions for the following question:
- What impression does this document give about Indian and British soldiers fighting together?

Exploring further

Use the teacher's notes to explain more about the role and contribution of Indian soldiers in the First World War. Tell the students they are now going to learn more about the experiences of these soldiers by listening to some short plays recorded as podcasts. The podcasts can be accessed at **https://media.nationalarchives.gov.uk/index.php/tag/loyalty-and-dissent**.

- *Corner of a Foreign Field:* Written by Hassan Abdulrazzak, this play begins with a conversation between Maulana Sadr Ud-Din and General Barrow, the Military Secretary to the India Office, about the appropriate burial grounds for Muslim soldiers.
- *Step Child:* Written by Amy Ng, this play is about the surveillance of Indian dissenters during the war.
- *Cama:* Written by Sharmila Chauhan, this play introduces Madame Cama, an important figure in the Indian Independence movement and explores loyalty and dissent during the First World War.
- *The Radicalisation of Vir Singh:* Written by Amman Paul Singh Brar, this play explores the challenges facing Arjun, a Sikh soldier.
- *Smile:* Written by Melanie Pennant, this play is about three Indian soldiers at the Brighton Pavilion Hospital.

Split the class into five groups and have each group listen to one of the plays. Each group can then report back to the rest of the class with the following:

- a short synopsis of the play
- a list of the characters in the play and their backgrounds
- what the play tells us about the experiences of people from South Asia in the First World War.

If preferred, you can print and hand out the transcripts of the plays available on the website. Or, you can choose one of the podcasts to listen to and discuss as a class.

Follow-up tasks
- Introduce students to some of the blog posts produced by the London School of Economics and Political Science on the South Asian contribution to the First World War: **https://blogs.lse.ac.uk/southasia/tag/first-world-war**.

LESSON 22

JEMADAR MIR DAST

> Jemadar Mir Dast, I.O.M., 55th Coke's Rifles (Frontier Force), attached 57th Wilde's Rifles (Frontier Force).
>
> For most conspicuous bravery and great ability at Ypres on 26th April, 1915, when he led his platoon with great gallantry during the attack, and afterwards collected various parties of the regiment (when no British Officers were left) and kept them under his command until the retirement was ordered.
>
> Jemadar Mir Dast subsequently on this day displayed remarkable courage in helping to carry eight British and Indian Officers into safety, whilst exposed to very heavy fire.

CONNECTION TO THE CURRICULUM

First World War 1914–1918 and Peace Settlement

Aim: To recognise the contribution of Indian servicemen in the First World War.

Historical figure: Jemadar Mir Dast (1874–1945)

Source: Report from *The London Gazette* (ZJ 1/622)

TEACHER'S NOTES

What is this source?

This is a report from *The London Gazette* newspaper on the actions of Jemadar Mir Dast, published on 29th June 1915.

What can we infer from this source?

We can infer quite a lot about the nature of trench warfare on the Western Front from the source. It gives a sense of the meaning of 'going over the top' to attack German lines whilst being 'exposed to very heavy fire'. During this attack gas was used, which would have added to the sense of confusion, injury and panic. Dast clearly kept control of his men and helped to carry eight injured men to safety whilst under heavy attack. We can infer that Dast was a courageous leader of men with strength of character. He led his own men in the attack and remained on the battlefield when 'no British officers were left' and others were retreating. We learn from the *Gazette* that Dast was an experienced soldier, previously decorated, and an officer.

Finally, the source shows that Indian troops served in the First World War as part of the Empire's army. This was not a war just fought by English 'Tommies' on the Western Front in France, but a vast army of collaborating forces who fought across the globe.

Why does The National Archives have this source?

The London Gazette is the official newspaper of the government. The *Gazette* included acts of state, proclamations and appointments under the Crown; also honours, decorations and medals; mentions in despatches or commendations; naval, military and Royal Air Force appointments and promotions.

What is the context of this source?

Mir Dast was a Pashtun born in Maidan, Tirah, now in modern-day Pakistan. He joined the British Army in 1894 and served before the war. He was promoted to the rank of jemadar in 1909, serving with the 55th Coke's Rifles and then on the Western Front with the 57th Wilde's Rifles from January 1915.

Over 1.3 million Indian soldiers served in the First World War, and over 74,000 lost their lives. These men came from modern-day India, Pakistan and Bangladesh. They fought from the start of the war at the First Battle of Ypres in November 1914 on the Western Front and in Egypt, Gallipoli, German East Africa and the Middle Eastern campaign in Mesopotamia, or were stationed to protect India's North-West Frontier. One hundred thousand Gurkhas served in the Indian Army and were also renowned for their bravery.

Like some other Indian soldiers, Mir Dast was sent to recover in the Royal Pavilion Hospital in Brighton. He was awarded the Victoria Cross in June 1915 for his service at the Second Battle of Ypres. He received his medal from George V. This is the highest military award for bravery in the face of the enemy and open to all members of the British armed forces regardless of rank. He was also promoted to the rank of *subedar*. He continued to suffer the effects of gas experienced during the attack and was invalided from the army; later he returned to India.

Today, a monument stands at the Memorial Gates at Hyde Park Corner in London to commemorate the Victoria Cross recipients of Indian heritage, including Mir Dast. In 2016, a blue plaque to commemorate Mir Dast was displayed at the India Gate in Brighton.

💡 LESSON IDEAS

ENQUIRY QUESTION
What can we learn about the contribution of Indian forces made during the First World War?

Getting started

Use this focus on Mir Dast to introduce the topic. The study could form part of a wider study on the role of the Indian Army in other theatres of the First World War.

Start by defining the key words in the document:

- jamadar (a junior officer rank of the Indian Army)
- I.O.M. (Indian Order of Merit)
- platoon
- regiment
- gallantry
- conspicuous.

Now use the teacher's notes to provide some context for the source.

Exploring further

Students can then become an expert on this source by reading and analysing it in detail. Use these questions to help:

- What type of source is this?
- What does it tell us about Mir Dast's career in the army?
- Where did Mir Dast see action in the First World War?
- What does it reveal about Mir Dast's actions on the battlefield?
- Can you describe the tone and language used in this source?
- What does it imply about his character?
- What does it suggest about his qualities as a leader of men?
- What others sources could be used to find out about Mir Dast's army career?

Follow-up tasks

- Record a podcast about the life of Mir Dast.
- Prepare a presentation with maps to show the contribution the Indian Army made in the different theatres of the First World War: Egypt, Gallipoli, German East Africa, Mesopotamia and guarding the North-West Frontier.
- Teachers can consult *The Indian Corps on the Western Front* by Simon Doherty and Tom Donovan for more detail on the role of the Indian Army in France and Belgium.

LESSON 23

EUAN LUCIE-SMITH

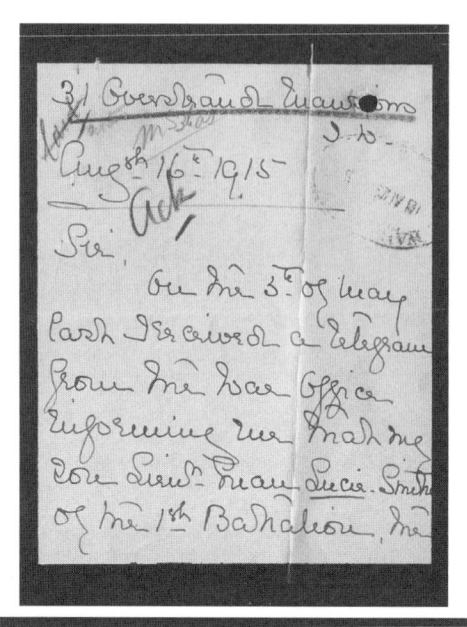

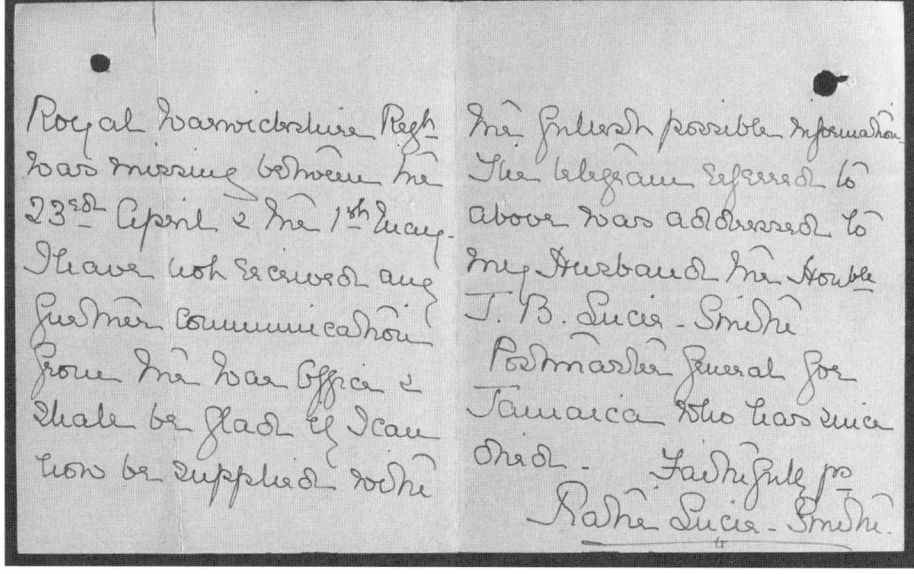

CONNECTION TO THE CURRICULUM

First World War 1914–1918 and Peace Settlement

Aim: To recognise the contribution of Black service men in the First World War.

Historical figure: Euan Lucie-Smith (1889–1915)

Source: Letter from Katie Lucie-Smith to the War Office (WO 339/10918)

TEACHER'S NOTES

What is this source?

This is a letter to the War Office from the mother of Euan Lucie-Smith, Lieutenant in the Royal Warwickshire Regiment, 1st Battalion. Katie Lucie-Smith is writing about her son who was reported missing between 25th April and 1st May 1915.

What can we infer from this source?

From the letter we can infer some details about Euan Lucie-Smith's parents and the social class of the family. His father is described as 'the Honourable' and was the Post Master General for Jamaica, meaning he ran the postal service in Jamaica. His wife Katie wrote that the telegram informing her that her son was missing was addressed to her husband. This suggests the subordinate position of women at the time.

Mrs Lucie-Smith has used mourning stationery because the paper is edged in black. The letter suggests that Katie Lucie-Smith was also an educated woman. The style of the letter is formal in tone. However, there is a definite sense of urgency and worry implied since she has received the telegram but no further news. The letter is addressed from Battersea in London, which suggests that Katie Lucie-Smith has left Jamaica and gone to England.

Why does The National Archives have this source?

This letter is contained in a file concerning an enquiry made by the British War Office on behalf of Katie Lucie-Smith about her son, who was declared missing in action in 1915.

What is the context of this source?

Euan Lucie-Smith was born in Jamaica. His father was the Honourable John Barkley Lucie-Smith and his mother was Lady Catherine Lucie-Smith. Euan was of mixed heritage. His father was a White civil servant and his mother the daughter of Jamaican lawyer and politician Samuel Constantine Burke. Euan was educated in England and joined the Jamaican Artillery Militia in 1911. At the start of the war, he was commissioned as a second lieutenant in the 1st Battalion, Royal Warwickshire Regiment.

Lucie-Smith was sent to France in March 1915 and died in April that year at the Second Battle of Ypres. He is commemorated on the Ploegsteert Memorial in Belgium. He was one of the first mixed-heritage infantry commissioned officers in a British Army regiment and the first Black officer to be killed in action in the First World War. It was previously thought that the first Black officer casualty was Walter Tull, killed in March 1918.

The file contains an earlier letter, dated 3rd May 1915, from Lady Lucie-Smith's other son stating that he and his mother intended to travel to England in June 1915. There is also a second letter from Katie Lucie-Smith, dated March 1916. She says that she has 'lately heard a rumour that there are several unidentified officers suffering from loss of memory and medical trouble caused by the war'. She asks the War Office about the location of these men and the particulars of the 'engagement her son was on 25th April'. She also asks for details about her other son.

Another record from the War Office from 21st February 1916 states: 'no further information can be given concerning this officer's fate'.

Diverse Histories © Clare Horrie and Rachel Hillman, 2022

💡 LESSON IDEAS

ENQUIRY QUESTION
What does this document reveal about the importance of Euan Lucie-Smith in the history of the First World War?

Getting started

Teachers can use this lesson to explore the contribution of Black servicemen during the First World War and it can be taught after Lesson 20 on Walter Tull.

Ask the students to imagine that this letter source has just been discovered and they are the historians who have been charged with becoming 'experts' on the source. What questions might they need to answer to help them investigate the source and take on this 'expert' role? Ask the class to brainstorm some questions and then work in groups to answer them.

Some suggestions include:

- What is the date of this letter?
- Who has written this letter?
- Why has this letter been written?
- What background details does it give about Euan Lucie-Smith?
- Why is there a black border on the letter?
- What does this letter reveal about the First World War?
- What other sources would help us find out more about Euan Lucie-Smith?

Exploring further

Ensure you have taught the lesson on Walter Tull and complete a short retrieval quiz with the students to assess what they can remember from this lesson. Reteach any key information they are missing.

The students can now create a parallel timeline showing the key events in the lives of Tull and Lucie-Smith, and compare and contrast the experiences of these two men.

The students then write a response to the essay question: 'What do the stories of Euan Lucie-Smith and Walter Tull tell us about the contribution of Black servicemen in the First World War?'

Follow-up tasks

- Students write a newspaper obituary for Euan Lucie-Smith with full details of his life, family, education and army career. They can find online the news story from October 2020, reported by *The Times*, about how Euan Lucie-Smith 'rewrote Black history of the First World War' to help with their research. (You could print out copies of this article for the students to read if you have access.)
- Teachers can consult *Black Poppies: Britain's Black Community and the Great War* by Stephen Bourne. This book explores the Black presence in Britain during and after the First World War, including the stories of Black servicemen of African heritage and Trinidadian soldier George A. Roberts.

LESSON 23
Euan Lucie-Smith

TRANSCRIPT

31 Overstand Mansions, S.W.

August 16th 1915

Sir

On the 5th of May last, I received a telegram from the War Office informing me that my son Euan Lucie-Smith of the 1st Battalion the Royal Warwickshire Regiment was missing between the 23rd April and the 1st May. I have not received any further communication from the War Office. I shall be glad if I can now be supplied to the fullest possible information. The telegram referred to above was addressed to my husband the Honourable J.B. Lucie-Smith, Post Master General for Jamaica who has since died.

Faithfully yours,

Katie Lucie-Smith

LESSON 24

CHINESE LABOUR CORPS IN THE FIRST WORLD WAR

'A' Company, 1st Battalion, prior to embarcation.

O.C.Battalion & N.C.O's on S.S.Teucer.

CONNECTION TO THE CURRICULUM

First World War 1914–1918 and Peace Settlement

Aim: To recognise the contribution of Chinese Labour Corps in the First World War.

Historical event: Chinese Labour Corps

Source: Two photographs of the Chinese Labour Corps (FO 371/2905 f.396, f.398)

TEACHER'S NOTES

What is this source?

These two photographs come from a Foreign Office file containing details about the Chinese Labour Corps (CLC) in 1917 first sent for duty in France.

What can we infer from this source?

Both photographs are inseparable from their original captions. They are records held by the Foreign Office to record the recruitment process of the CLC. The first photograph shows 'A' Company, 1st Battalion. The term 'company' can mean a few dozen to 200 soldiers. They are pictured outside a building, probably one of the barracks set up to receive the recruits before their embarkation on the *SS Teucer* (second picture). The man leading the group is not dressed in military uniform. Perhaps he is an official involved in the recruitment process or a British military official.

The second photograph shows non-commissioned officers who supervised the labour corps. It shows some of the CLC on board the *SS Teucer* at the start of their journey to France. The photographs are significant because the role of the CLC has largely been forgotten in histories of the First World War.

Why does The National Archives have this source?

This is a Foreign Office file containing details about the CLC in 1917.

What is the context of this source?

The First World War was waged on an industrial scale and necessitated a range of services to supply and support the frontline. At the start of the war, certain Pioneer Battalions, when not fighting in the trenches on the Western Front, were used for this work. By 1916, after a huge loss of men, it was clear that a dedicated labour force was needed.

The British recruited Chinese workers to form the CLC to work behind the lines. They had also used vast numbers of colonial workers from India, South Africa and Egypt, both in France and the Middle East. Recruitment started in 1916 in Wei-Hai-Wei, a British-leased territory. In January 1917, 1,086 men of the 1st Battalion of the CLC left for France.

In France, the CLC dug trenches, repaired roads and railway lines, and moved supplies. Further from the front, they worked in ports, mines and factories making munitions or cutting wood in forests. After the war, they filled in trenches and recovered the dead. Their working conditions were brutal. Some died during the fighting from falling shells or the flu pandemic. By the time of the armistice in 1918, there were about 195 Chinese Labour companies, representing a total of 95,500 Chinese labourers.

According to a War Office document 'Chinese labour was undoubtedly most efficient, the extensive system of defence organised in [the] rear at the time of the enemy offensive in 1918 could not have been completed in the time if not for the excellent work of the C.L.C.' It is shocking that the contribution made by the CLC has largely been forgotten. 2,000 members of the CLC, described as war casualties, were buried in graveyards in the north of France and Belgium. However, no permanent memorial to the CLC was created in Britain.

💡 LESSON IDEAS

ENQUIRY QUESTION
What do these photographs reveal about the importance of Chinese Labour Corps in the history of the First World War?

Getting started

Teachers can use this lesson to explore the Chinese Labour Corps during the First World War. The story of these men and their bravery has remained hidden in many histories of the First World War and has only been recently recognised.

In order to encourage your students to develop their observational skills for the interpretation of these sources, introduce each photograph using the 'five-second rule'. Give the class just five seconds to look at it on a whiteboard or printout. Ask them to remember anything they notice. Repeat a second time, but give them ten seconds to view it. What else have they noticed?

Exploring further

Now reveal the image for five to ten minutes and ask the students to jot down all the points they can make about the source. Suggested prompt questions for discussion include:

- Why were these photographs taken?
- What is the value of their captions?
- Why are these photographs significant to historians?
- What arrangements for the new Chinese recruits would have been made before departing on *SS Teucer*, do you think?
- How could we use the information provided by the photographs for further research into the Chinese Labour Corps?

Encourage the students to share their answers in discussion for the enquiry question: What do these photographs reveal about the importance of Chinese Labour Corps in the history of the First World War?

Students can then write a report on the role of the Chinese Labour Corps, including a map of how they travelled to France, details of the work they did behind the lines, what happened to them after the war and during the flu pandemic of 1918.

Follow-up tasks

- Students can research other photographs of the CLC at the Imperial War Museum. What more can they learn from these photographs that the sources provided in the lesson don't show?
- Support students to find out how and where the CLC are commemorated in the battlefields of France and Belgium and explore the *Ensuring We Remember Campaign*.
- Teachers can consult *Harry Livingstone's Forgotten Men: Canadians and the Chinese Labour Corps in the First World War* by Dan Black for more information.

LESSON 25

INDIAN LABOUR CORPS IN THE FIRST WORLD WAR

> (f) Work.
>
> The great majority of Indian Companies were sent up to the Third Army Area on their arrival, and most of them were employed to begin with on Salvage in the then Special Salvage Area. They very soon finished up the work, and proved most useful, hardworking and willing.
>
> Most of the men were earth workers, but quickly adapted themselves to the different tasks on which they were put.

CONNECTION TO THE CURRICULUM

First World War 1914–1918 and Peace Settlement

Aim: To recognise the contribution of the Indian Labour Corps in France.

Historical event: Indian Labour Corps

Source: Extract from a War Office report on the labour force of the British Expeditionary Force (WO 107/37)

Caution: This source contains language that is inappropriate and unacceptable today.

TEACHER'S NOTES

What is this source?

This extract comes from a War Office report from November 1919 on the labour force of the British Expeditionary Force (BEF) during the First World War. This extract relates to the Indian Labour Corps (ILC).

What can we infer from this source?

We can infer that this extract is part of a larger report. This is an item labelled '(f)'. It is typed and seems official. It would be read by other army officials and was produced in 1919 at the end of the war. This extract is an account of the role played by the Indian labour companies. The majority of the ILC were attached to the Third Army. They were mostly involved in salvage to begin with. Salvage work meant clearing abandoned items, such as equipment near the trenches. The ILC were called 'earth workers'. The extract suggests that they are willing, hard workers, that they take orders and are slight in build.

Why does The National Archives have this source?

The report was held and created by the War Office.

What is the context of this source?

The First World War necessitated services to supply and support those at the front with ammunition and supplies through a system of transport, ports, depots and workshops. A large workforce was essential to achieve victory. The British Indian government agreed in 1917 to send 50,000 ILC workers to France. According to the War Office report containing our extract, the first contingent of the ILC arrived in Marseilles on 16th June 1917.

The various labour corps had been recruited in India from Binar and Orisea, Assam, North-West Frontier, Burma and Bengal. Each corps consisted of four sections of 480 men. Once the ILC had settled in, 'urgent orders for supplies and ammunition from the Base Depots were many, but the Indians could be relied upon to turn out, even though they had completed a day's heavy work in order to help beat the enemy.'

Indian labourers were often used closer to the frontlines on fortification work. The No. 65 and 66 Manipur Labour Companies were praised for their 'excellent semi-skilled work in making trench boards, camp construction work, etc., thereby relieving personnel in more forward areas'. Other sections of the ILC were involved in salvage, roadmaking, quarrying and brickmaking. The work was back-breaking.

The report of the role of the ILC said: 'Some of the Companies did splendid work and during the German offensive in March, 1918, all Indian units without exception behaved in an admirable manner…there was no panic, although in some cases the companies had to endure shell fire and attacks from aeroplanes with bombs and machine guns, both by day and night'. They also continued to load trains and one company assisted with a special hospital train and helped the wounded, gaining high praise from medical officers.

A total of 1,174 men who died while serving with the ILC are commemorated on the India Gate memorial in New Delhi. The Indian Memorial at Neuve Chapelle in France commemorates over 4,700 Indian soldiers *and* labourers who lost their lives on the Western Front during the First World War.

💡 LESSON IDEAS

ENQUIRY QUESTION
What does this source reveal about the importance of Indian Labour Corps on the Western Front?

Getting started

Use this lesson to explore the role of the Indian Labour Corps in France before studying how they contributed in other theatres of the First World War. This lesson can be used in conjunction with Lessons 21 and 22, which concern soldiers from South Asia who fought in the First World War.

Show the students the source and give them some time to read it. Ask the students to become 'experts' on this source. What questions might they need to investigate to understand the source and assess its value to the enquiry? Ask the class to brainstorm some questions together and write them on the board.

Exploring further

The students can then work in groups to answer the questions on the board. You might need to define some terms using the teacher's notes. Take particular care with the term 'coolie' and ensure the students understand that this is a deeply offensive term and not appropriate to use.

Some questions the students might have come up with are listed below. If the students have missed any of these questions, you could use them to develop the discussion further.

- What is this document?
- Why has it been created?
- Why does the War Office have it?
- What is the role of the Indian Labour Corps according to the source?
- How are the Indian Labour Corps viewed in this document?
- Is this source sufficient to find out about the role of the Indian Labour Corps?

Finally, discuss how to find out more about the other work carried out by the Indian Labour Corps.

Follow-up tasks

- As a homework task, ask students to explore some of the avenues for further information they have come up with to find out more about the Indian Labour Corps. They can then write an account on the role of the Indian Labour Corps in France, including details of the work they did behind the lines.
- Two Indian Labour Corps units were formed in 1915 to take part in the Gallipoli Campaign. They also served in the Mesopotamian Campaign, Persia and the Salonika Campaign in Greece. Ask the students to locate these on a map and find out about their work.
- Teachers can consult *No Labour, No Battle: Military Labour During the First World War* by John Starling and Ivor Lee, for more information.

LESSON 26

THE 1919 RACE RIOTS

> **Cardiff City Police.**
>
> TELEPHONE No 3213.
>
> Reference
>
> Head Quarters,
> Law Courts.
>
> (5)
>
> comprising 16 coloured men for shooting; one coloured man for possessing firearms; and 4 Britishers for wilful damage. The casualties were approximately 12 in number; two proved fatal (one white and one coloured man) 3 coloured men have fractured skulls; one white man fractured skull; and the others were minor injuries.
>
> It is not possible for me to estimate in figures the damage that has been caused.
>
> So far as this day, Friday, has gone there is a certain liveliness amongst the white population in and abutting upon the affected area. It may develop during the evening but I have increased the mounted police on duty to 12 in number and am practically concentrating all my Force in the area of Butetown which is approximately a mile long by 300 yards wide.
>
> There can be no doubt that the aggressors have been those belonging to the white race. To go fully into the probable cause of their attitude would open up many issues but briefly it might safely be said that racial feeling which now exists is due to the following:-
>
> The coloured men resent their inability to secure employment on ships since the Armistice as they are being displaced by white crews;
>
> They are dissatisfied with the action of the Government;
>
> They regard themselves as British subjects;
>
> They claim equal treatment with whites and contend that they fought for the British Empire during the war and manned their food ships during the submarine campaign.
>
> The white population appear to be alarmed at the association of so many white women with the coloured races and imagine that they entice the white women to their houses. (As a matter of fact so far as the Police can observe certain white women court the favour of the coloured races).
>
> The housing question also arises. The coloured men have earned good wages during the war; they have saved their money; they have purchased houses; are always willing to pay higher rents; and even exhorbitant sums as "key money" to secure possession of dwelling houses or shop premises. This feature particularly irritates the demobilized soldiers who have been unable to secure housing accommodation.

CONNECTION TO THE CURRICULUM

Challenges for Britain, Europe and the wider world: 1901 to the present day

Aim: To find out about race relations in post-war Britain.

Historical event: The 1919 Race Riots

Source: Extract of a letter written by Cardiff's Chief Constable to the Under Secretary of State on 13th June 1919 (HO 45/11017/3776969)

Caution: This source contains language that is inappropriate and unacceptable today.

📖 TEACHER'S NOTES

What is this source?

This is an extract of a letter written by Cardiff's Chief Constable to the Under Secretary of State on 13th June 1919. It is held within a Home Office file entitled 'ALIENS: Repatriation of Coloured Seamen etc.' The word 'aliens' refers to people not classed as citizens or nationals of the UK. Today using 'alien' to describe immigrants is seen as dehumanising and derogatory.

What can we infer from this source?

This document is the fifth page of a longer document – indicated by the number '5' in brackets at the top. It has been typewritten, which helps to date it, and it is typed on headed paper from the Cardiff City Police. These details tell us that the writer is from the police force and this is a formal document being sent to another person or organisation.

Once you start to read the contents of this document, it quickly becomes clear that the writer is describing serious events that have involved both 'coloured' and 'white' men. The 'coloured' men are described as having been in possession of firearms, whilst the 'Britishers' have caused 'wilful damage', although it's not clear if they also had guns or weapons. A number of people have been hurt, two fatally – 'one white and one coloured man' – and the writer also implies that there has been much damage to property too.

The writer goes on to talk specifically about Butetown where he is concentrating 'all my force', suggesting that he must be senior within the Cardiff City Police. He writes about the 'white population' as being the 'aggressors', implying that they initiated this conflict. However, the writer then says that he thinks there are a number of reasons to explain why this feeling exists. The writer refers to the feelings of both groups. He describes the 'white people' disliking the inter-racial relationships that are taking place, and the fact that many of the 'coloured men' have earned good wages during the war.

In contrast, the writer lists the 'coloured men's' resentment at losing their jobs to White crews onboard ships. This appears to be in direct reference to the repatriation scheme launched by the government in February 1919 in British seaports, to return Arab and Black colonial workers to their country of origin.

Why does The National Archives have this source?

This document is held within a Home Office file.

What is the context of this source?

After the end of the First World War, millions of people were faced with unemployment and a shortage of housing. In port towns across the country, many White people, angry at the lack of jobs, blamed ethnic and minority communities whose numbers had grown during the war. Yet there were already established Black and ethnic minority communities settled in Cardiff before the war, as evident in the 1911 census.

On 11th June in Cardiff, conflict ensued between White men and local Butetown communities of Yemeni, Somali and Afro-Caribbean backgrounds. Riots lasted for three days before dying down. Other violent riots occurred in places including Glasgow, Hull, London, Newport, Barry and Liverpool.

Diverse Histories © Clare Horrie and Rachel Hillman, 2022

💡 LESSON IDEAS

ENQUIRY QUESTION
What does this document reveal about race relations in Britain in 1919?

Getting started

Use this document as part of your work to introduce students to post-First World War Britain and race relations at this time.

Ask the students to look at the appearance of the document for thirty seconds. Ask the following questions:

- What type of document do you think it is? Why?
- Where do you think it has come from?
- Is it the full document?

Ask them to explain their answers.

Exploring further

Give the students time to read the document properly and think about the following questions:

- What type of document do you think it is now?
- What information can you glean about the author?
- What events have taken place?
- How does the author explain the reasons for these events?

Bring the students' answers together in a class discussion about what this document reveals about Britain and race relations after the First World War.

Provide students with further details and context about the 1919 Race Riots using the teacher's notes. Show them this video from The Black Curriculum as a summary of the information: **www.youtube.com/watch?v=AQ2HmVsQCIo**. Can the students plan and storyboard their own short video about the riots based on what they now know about these events?

Follow-up tasks

- Introduce students to documents relating to events that occurred in other places as part of the 1919 unrest. Were all these events driven by ethnicity? The National Archives website has an excellent resource containing documents that can be used for this activity. See: **www.nationalarchives.gov.uk/education/resources/1919-race-riots**.
- Introduce students to the work of historian Jacqueline Jenkinson, the author of *Black 1919*, which looks at the motivations and make-up of the rioters and how the police responded to events.

LESSON 27

MASSACRE IN AMRITSAR

CONNECTION TO THE CURRICULUM

Challenges for Britain, Europe and the wider world: 1901 to the present day

Aim: To investigate how the British Raj responded to events in Amritsar.

Historical figure: General Dyer

Source: Extracts from an enquiry report dated 20th April 1920 (PRO 30/30/18, page 7)

TEACHER'S NOTES

What is this source?

The extracts come from a report produced by a committee of enquiry appointed by the Governor General of India and the Secretary of State to investigate disturbances in Bombay, Delhi and the Punjab. The committee was headed by Lord Hunter.

What can we infer from the source extracts?

The first extract details events at Jallianwala Bagh and the actions of General Dyer. The report criticises him for firing without warning at the assembled crowd and continuing to fire until the crowd dispersed. We can infer that the committee have interviewed Dyer to gather evidence about events. He stated that 'his mind was made up before he came along' and he was going to 'fire at once'. The report criticised Dyer for not sufficiently warning people against assembling. He is condemned for his military judgement and wanting to 'create a moral effect throughout the Punjab'. He did not save the area from a second 'mutiny' and failed to attend to the wounded. Although the Committee seems to have accepted that 'he had a very small force' and nobody asked him to help.

The 'Mutiny' mentioned refers to the so-called 'Indian Mutiny' also known as the Sepoy Mutiny, the Indian Rebellion 1857 or the First War of Independence. It was a widespread but unsuccessful uprising against British rule in India from 1857 to 1859.

We can infer from the second extract that a minority do not agree with 'the majority' that the crowd would only have dispersed if fired at. Instead, they believe that Dyer thought 'that India must be ruled by force'. This minority are also critical of the Punjab government, the British Raj, in failing to gather details of the number who died.

Why does The National Archives have this source?

These papers relate to the Indian Disorders Committee (Jallianwala Bagh, Amritsar).

What is the context?

After the First World War, India faced a deep economic recession and unemployment rose. Around 13 million people died in the Spanish influenza pandemic and poor harvests led to famine. The British government in India feared the spread of Bolshevism and the Raj introduced the Rowlatt Acts in 1919. The Rowlatt Acts were opposed throughout India. In Amritsar, buildings were burnt and Europeans were attacked. Sir Michael O'Dwyer, Governor of the Punjab, ordered General Dyer there on 13th April. A political meeting was planned at Jallianwala Bagh to discuss the Rowlatt Acts. When Dyer first entered Amritsar in the morning, a proclamation was read out declaring a curfew.

Dyer led a troop of 50 riflemen of the 9th Gurkhas, 54th Sikhs and 59th Sikhs to Jallianwala Bagh. A peaceful crowd of 20,000 had gathered there against the meeting ban. In a shocking act of brutality, Dyer ordered his men to fire immediately.

Events at Amritsar exposed Britain's promises of self-government as hollow. It strengthened contempt for the Raj and stirred nationalist feeling across India. Gandhi began organising his first campaign for mass civil disobedience against British rule in the bid for full independence.

Diverse Histories © Clare Horrie and Rachel Hillman, 2022

💡 LESSON IDEAS

ENQUIRY QUESTION
How did the British Raj respond to events at Amritsar?

Getting started

Use this source to introduce events at Amritsar as part of a wider investigation into the history of India after the First World War, including:

- recession
- Spanish flu pandemic
- Government of India Act
- Rowlatt Acts
- the crisis point of Amritsar
- the reaction of the British government and public.

Ensure any difficult vocabulary in the source is defined before the class look at it. Explain that Jallianwala Bagh was a wasteland area surrounded by low walls and had several entrances. It was in the city of Amritsar, located in the Punjab region of India, which was under British rule.

Read the source through together. Use a highlighter on the whiteboard or printout to show the key points.

Exploring further

Once you have finished reading through the document and students have a good sense of the context of the source, ask them to discuss the following questions in pairs:

- Why was this source created?
- How do you think the committee compiled the information contained in this report?

- Can you find out what was the impact of events at Amritsar on: (a) Indians (b) the British Raj?
- Can you find out how General Dyer was treated after his actions at Amritsar? How did the British government and public respond?

Follow-up tasks

- Students can conduct some research in order to write a profile of:
  - Michael O'Dwyer, Governor of Punjab
  - Gandhi and the civil disobedience campaign against British rule and the independence movement.
- Students can draw a map of India around 1900, showing British India (the Raj) and the Princely states (indigenous rulers who had internal control but the British controlled their foreign policy).
- Teachers can consult the following resource for a range of portraits of historical figures, political cartoons, newspapers, photographs, propaganda posters and eyewitness accounts: *Eyewitness at Amritsar: A Visual History of the 1919 Jallianwala Bagh Massacre* by Amandeep Singh Madr.

LESSON 28

THE BRITISH EMPIRE IN THE 1920s

THE EMPIRE CHRISTMAS PUDDING
according to the recipe supplied by the King's Chef Mr. CEDARD, with Their Majesties' Gracious Consent

Ingredient	Origin
1 lb Currants	Australia
1 lb Sultanas	Australia or South Africa
1 lb Stoned Raisins	Australia or South Africa
5 ozs Minced Apple	United Kingdom or Canada
1 lb Bread Crumbs	United Kingdom
1 lb Beef Suet	United Kingdom
6½ ozs Cut Candied Peel	South Africa
8 ozs Flour	United Kingdom
8 ozs Demerara Sugar	British West Indies or British Guiana
5 Eggs	United Kingdom or Irish Free State
½ oz Ground Cinnamon	India or Ceylon
¼ oz Ground Cloves	Zanzibar
¼ oz Ground Nutmegs	British West Indies
¼ teaspoon Pudding Spice	India or British West Indies
¼ gill Brandy	Australia · S. Africa Cyprus or Palestine
½ gill Rum	Jamaica or British Guiana
1 pint Beer	England · Wales · Scotland or Ireland

WRITE TO THE EMPIRE MARKETING BOARD, WESTMINSTER, FOR A FREE BOOKLET ON EMPIRE CHRISTMAS FARE GIVING THIS AND OTHER RECIPES.

> **CONNECTION TO THE CURRICULUM**
> Challenges for Britain, Europe and the wider world: 1901 to the present day
> **Aim:** To understand how Britain traded within the Empire.
> **Historical event:** British Empire in the 1920s
> **Source:** Poster from the Empire Marketing Board (CO 956/63)

TEACHER'S NOTES

What is this source?

This is a poster from the Empire Marketing Board (EMB). The EMB was set up by the government in 1926, for carrying out research, marketing and publicity. The aim was to improve the markets for British and colonial products. It was chaired by the Secretary of State for the Colonies and worked with advertisers and artists to create posters to encourage trade within the Empire.

What can we infer from this source?

The poster suggests that the British Empire was a global community because the ingredients needed to make the 'Empire Christmas pudding' come from all parts of the Empire. It was produced by the EMB which, by its very name, would suggest an interest in promoting trade within the Empire. The EMB would have wanted British people to buy Empire goods and vice versa, and foster good relations at home and abroad. The Empire board is trying to influence shopping habits, in particular at Christmas time. People can also write to them to get other recipes, which in turn would encourage them to buy Empire products.

Why does The National Archives have this source?

The poster is part of a collection produced by the EMB. It is found in the Colonial Office collection.

What is the context of this source?

As part of the EMB's marketing campaign, another poster was produced called 'Making the Empire Christmas pudding'. This colourful poster shows a woman making Christmas pudding surrounded by ingredients including 'Jamaican Rum', other spices to represent the colonies, and 'John Bull shredded suet' to represent the mother country. Thus the posters of EMB often visualised the home country with its colonies to suggest a feeling of community. Two other posters in the series, also produced in 1927, focus on India. The first points out that Britain imports £66,000,000 worth of Indian goods and the other that India imports £86,000,000 worth of British goods.

At this time, the British Empire was at its most extensive. During both world wars the colonies contributed huge numbers of men, women and resources, but after 1945 the British Empire declined as independence movements continued to take root. By the late 1960s, most of Britain's colonies had become independent countries. The majority still keep their ties with Britain through the Commonwealth.

💡 LESSON IDEAS

ENQUIRY QUESTION
What does this source reveal about the British Empire by the 1920s?

Getting started

Use this source to extend the knowledge gained in Lesson 18 on the British Empire in the time of Queen Victoria. How extensive was the Empire by the 1920s?

Introduce the source using the 'five-second rule'. Give the class just five seconds to look at it. Ask them to remember anything they notice. Repeat a second time, but give them ten seconds to view it. What else have they noticed?

Exploring further

Now reveal the image for five to ten minutes and ask the students to jot down all the points they can make about the source, then share in discussion to draw conclusions for the enquiry question. You might want to provide some prompt questions:

- What type of source is this?
- How many countries are in the British Empire?
- How does the poster use a recipe for Christmas pudding to show the size of the British Empire?
- What do you think is the message of this poster?
- Why do you think it was produced?
- What is the Empire Marketing Board?

Tell the students more about the additional sources mentioned in the teacher's notes to contextualise the original source further. Explain that the British Empire was at its most extensive in the 1920s and the colonies contributed significantly to both world wars. You can then go on to explore what happened after 1945, when the British Empire began declining.

Follow-up tasks ✏️

- Create an illustrated leaflet which explains what 'Dominion status' meant for some nations in the British Empire in the 1920s. When did they became independent?
- Write a presentation on the formation of the Commonwealth of Nations.
- Write a report explaining how and why Hong Kong was returned to China in 1997.

LESSON 29

SHAPURJI SAKLATVALA MP

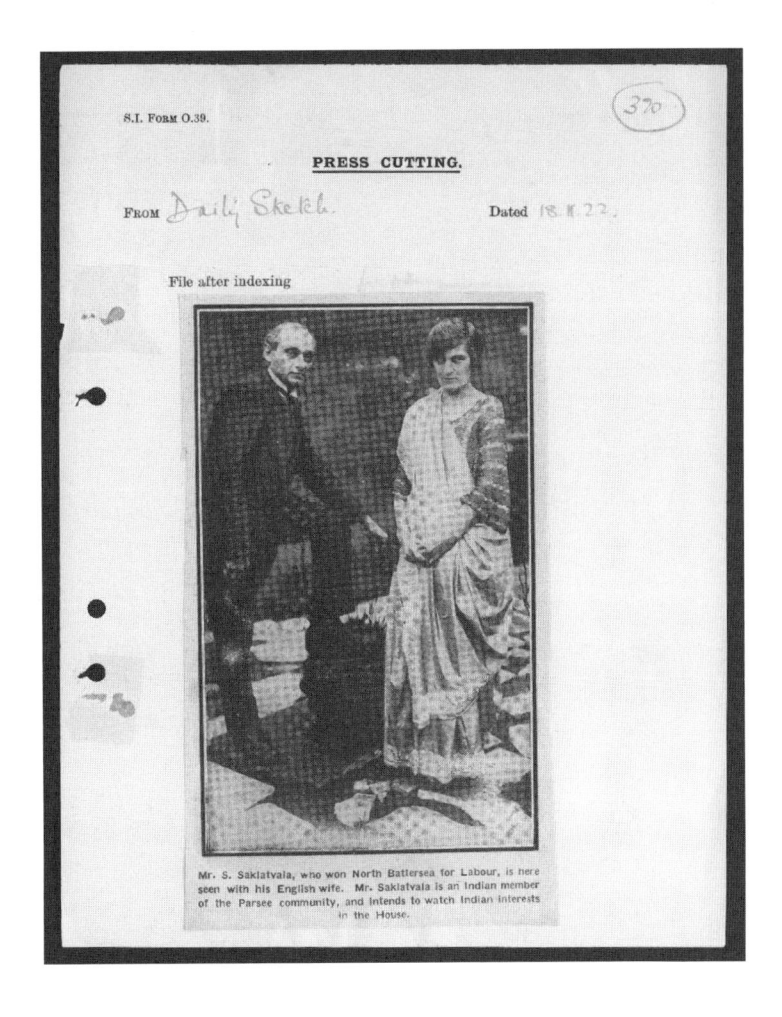

> **CONNECTION TO THE CURRICULUM**
> Challenges for Britain, Europe and the wider world: 1901 to the present day
> **Aim:** To explore the political significance of Shapurji Saklatvala.
> **Historical figure:** Shapurji Saklatvala (1874–1936)
> **Source:** Press cutting from the Daily Sketch (KV 2/614)

TEACHER'S NOTES

What is this source?

This is a press cutting from a security service file on Shapurji Saklatvala, who was an MP of South Asian heritage in the 1920s.

What can we infer from this source?

As the source comes from a security services file it suggests it was part of an information gathering exercise on the activities of Shapurji Saklatvala. The newspaper clipping comes from the *Daily Sketch* and is dated 18th December 1922. The *Sketch* was a conservative paper, popularist in tone, aiming to appeal to 'the man in the street' rather than those in power.

The caption says Shapurji Saklatvala intended to 'watch Indian interests in the House' and seems to suggest the fear that Shapurji Saklatvala would campaign in Parliament on Indian concerns. These might have included raising questions about working conditions for Indian sailors and others, or speaking out against the British Raj in India. The caption refers to his 'English wife'. Does this suggest interracial marriages were considered newsworthy at the time or something more?

Why does The National Archives have it?

The source comes from the British government's security services records. This series contains files on suspected spies, renegades, Communist sympathisers and anti-conscription groups.

What is the context of this source?

The file also contains a page which has been extracted from the 'MI5 "Black List" Volume XXI (Indian Volume)'. This provides information about Saklatvala's activities. It would appear that he was somebody whom the security services intended to watch as they had placed him on a 'Black List'. Such concerns are implied by comments in this document which recorded that 'since 1918 up to the present time, he has been one of the most prominent of India agitators in England and he has long been connected with all the principal Socialist, Bolshevik and anti-British societies'. These comments should be viewed in the context of Britain's hostility to the Indian struggle for independence, the impact of the massacre at Amritsar and the international impact of the Russian Revolution in 1917. We also learn from this extract that in 1920 Saklatvala's house was raided and his papers seized.

Saklatvala was the son of Dorabji Shapurji Saklatvala and nephew of Sir Raban Tata. He came to England in 1905 and lived in Manchester where he managed the Tata company office. In 1909 Saklatvala joined the Independent Labour Party and the Indian Home Rule League, founded in 1916. In 1917 he became a founder member of the Workers' Welfare League. He became the Labour candidate for Battersea North in 1921.

He won the Battersea seat in 1922, which he lost the following year. He stood again in 1924 as the Communist candidate and won, holding the seat until 1929. He supported the General Strike in 1926. Saklatvala was also a great supporter of Indian students in London. Saklatvala was the third Member of Parliament of South Asian heritage in Britain; the first was Dadabha Naoroji in 1894, the Liberal MP for Finsbury.

💡 LESSON IDEAS

ENQUIRY QUESTION
What does this document reveal about the political significance of Shapurji Saklatvala after the First World War?

Getting started

Teachers can use this lesson to examine the document and teach the students more about Shapurji Saklatvala. Students take turns to become an 'expert' on this secret document source just released by The National Archives. Use these questions to prompt discussion:

- What is the date of this document?
- What type of source is this?
- Who has created this document?
- Why has this information been gathered?
- What does it reveal about Shapurji Saklatvala?
- How can we tell this photograph is posed?
- Comment on the language and tone of the caption. What does it suggest?
- Can you find out the meaning of the term 'Parsee community'?
- What does this secret source reveal about the concerns of the British government?
- What other sources would help us find out more about Shapurji Saklatvala?

Exploring further

The students can then use what they have learned from the source and any further information you have given them about Shapurji Saklatvala to write a newspaper obituary for Saklatvala, with full details of his life and his work as an MP.

Follow-up tasks

- Students make a glossary for the following organisations in the 1920s: Communist Party, Independent Labour Party, India Home Rule League, Workers' Welfare League, League against Imperialism, MI5.
- Teachers or students can use the Open University web resource, Making Britain, to find out about other individuals of South Asian heritage in British history from 1870 to 1950. See: **www.open.ac.uk/researchprojects/makingbritain.**

LESSON 30

MARCUS GARVEY IN BRITAIN

> Tickets (incld. tax), 12s., 5s. 9d., 3s.
> LIONEL POWELL, 161, NEW BOND-STREET, W. 1.
>
> ROYAL ALBERT HALL,
> KENSINGTON GORE, S.W.
> WEDNESDAY EVENING, June 6th, 8 o'clock.
>
> A MIGHTY REVELATION!
> The Historic Appearance of
> **MARCUS GARVEY.**
>
> The World's Greatest Orator and Negro Leader. He shall speak to the White Race as never man spoke before on behalf of the Black Peoples of the World.
>
> Supported by an excellent Concert Programme contributed to by African, American, and West Indian Negro Artistes.
>
> **ETHYL OUGHTON CLARKE,**
> Celebrated Negro Soprano of the United States, will appear.
>
> ORCHESTRAL MUSIC.
>
> Hear and see the man who has left America wondering.
>
> Every thoughtful white person will hear this man, one of the rare personalities of our Age.
> ADMISSION (Including Tax): Stalls, 5s. 9d.; Arena, 4s. 9d.; Orchestra, 4s. 6d.; Gallery, 1s. 2d.; Box Seats, 4s. 9d. each. Tickets on sale, Box Office, Royal Albert Hall.

> **CONNECTION TO THE CURRICULUM**
>
> Challenges for Britain, Europe and the wider world: 1901 to the present day
>
> **Aim:** To find out about Marcus Garvey, Pan-Africanist leader and campaigner.
>
> **Historical figure:** Marcus Garvey (1887–1940)
>
> **Source:** Newspaper advertisement for an appearance of Marcus Garvey (CO 554/78/8)
>
> **Caution:** This source contains language that is inappropriate and unacceptable today.

TEACHER'S NOTES

What is this source?

This source is taken from a Colonial Office file entitled: 'Activities of Marcus Garvey and the Universal Negro Improvement Association', 1928. The source is a newspaper clipping held in the file, but there is no indication in which newspaper the advertisement appeared.

What can we infer from this source?

We can infer from the source that Marcus Garvey, Pan-Africanist leader and campaigner, was visiting London to speak at the Royal Albert Hall in June 1928. The event was supported by a performance from African, American and West Indian artists, including Ethyl Oughton Clarke, famous soprano, and other orchestral music. Details of ticket prices and time of performance are given. The Royal Albert Hall is a very well-known, important venue. We can infer from the advertisement that this was going to be a significant Black cultural event. The tone and persuasive language of the short advert certainly suggests this. Marcus Garvey's appearance is described in block capitals as 'a mighty revelation' and 'historic'. It suggests the evening is going to be thought-provoking and challenging as this is a man who has left America 'wondering'. There is a call for 'every thoughtful white person' to listen to him as 'one of the rare personalities of our age'.

Why does The National Archives have this source?

This newspaper clipping appears in a Colonial Office file entitled: 'Activities of Marcus Garvey and the Universal Negro Improvement Association', 1928.

What is the context of this source?

Marcus Garvey, born in Jamaica in 1887, was a Pan-Africanist. His ideas strongly influenced Black politics, including Black Power, national liberation movements, and Rastafarianism.

One of 11 children, he left school at 14 to work as a printer's apprentice. As a young man he travelled around South America. In 1914 he founded the hugely successful Universal Negro Improvement Association and then in 1916 moved to New York. The movement called people of African descent to have racial pride and aspire to cultural and economic independence. It had millions of members across the world, notably in the USA, Africa, the Caribbean and Britain. Garvey declared himself Provisional President of Africa. He campaigned for Africa to be decolonised and united as a single political entity.

Garvey, a powerful orator, toured all over North America calling African Americans to reclaim their homeland as part of the Back-to-Africa movement to celebrate their race and return to Africa. In 1919 he founded the Black Star shipping line to support relocation to Africa. He approached the West African government of Liberia to donate land for resettlement, but this was refused. The Black Star line collapsed in 1922 and Garvey was prosecuted for fraud and later deported to Jamaica where he remained.

Garvey's ideas about racial separatism and the return to Africa were not shared by other African American Pan-Africanist activists like W.E.B. Du Bois. From 1935 Marcus Garvey spent the rest of his life in Britain, where he died. He is commemorated with a blue plaque at Talgarth Road, Hammersmith in London.

💡 LESSON IDEAS

ENQUIRY QUESTION
What does this source reveal about the significance of Marcus Garvey?

Getting started

Use this source to introduce Marcus Garvey, Black nationalist and civil rights campaigner. The lesson should form part of a wider investigation into the history of the British Black Power movement, decolonisation and human rights.

Ensure students have some basic information and context about Marcus Garvey before introducing the source. Present students with the source and ask them to read it. Students should then jot down four significant points about this source.

Exploring further

Ask the students to share some of the points they have written down. Draw out the key information that can be inferred from the source in a class discussion.

- Why do the students think the source was created?
- What is it advertising?
- What does it reveal about Marcus Garvey?
- What other sources could we use to find out about Marcus Garvey?

Teachers could discuss extracts of the speech given by Marcus Garvey advertised in the source, which is located on the British Library website: **www.bl.uk/collection-items/report-of-a-speech-delivered-by-marcus-garvey-6th-june-1928**.

> **Follow-up tasks**
> - Write a profile or chronology on the life of Marcus Garvey.
> - Produce a slideshow about the Universal Negro Improvement Association.

LESSON 31

THE LEAGUE OF COLOURED PEOPLES

OBJECTS:

To promote and protect the Social, Educational, Economic and Political interests of its members.

To interest members in the welfare of Coloured Peoples in all parts of the world.

To improve relations between the races.

To co-operate and affiliate with organisations sympathetic to Coloured People.

CONNECTION TO THE CURRICULUM

Challenges for Britain, Europe and the wider world: 1901 to the present day

Aim: To find out about organisations in Britain campaigning for Black civil rights in the 1930s and 1940s.

Historical group: The League of Coloured Peoples (1931–1951)

Source: Extract from a document published by The League of Coloured Peoples (CO 321/369/3)

Caution: This source contains language that is inappropriate and unacceptable today.

TEACHER'S NOTES

What is this source?

This is an extract of headed paper from The League of Coloured Peoples, stating their aims as an organisation. It is held within Colonial Office files regarding 'seditious' publications and 'The Protest by the Coloured Peoples League against censorship'.

What can we infer from this source?

This is an extract from a longer document. It is written in printed text and sets out four 'objects' or aims. The first two aims refer to its 'members', suggesting that these aims belong to an organisation with a specific membership. The first aim states that it wants to improve and protect the status and interests of its members in social, economic, educational and political terms. The second and fourth aims use the term 'Coloured Peoples' with regards to their welfare (wellbeing) and the organisation's motivation to work with other groups who are 'sympathetic' to 'coloured people'. This suggests that the document has been written a number of years ago; the use of the term 'coloured' today is not an acceptable way to describe people's ethnicity, but was used from the mid-nineteenth century onwards and into the 1930s and 1940s.

It also suggests that the organisation itself is made up of 'coloured people' who are looking to work with other similar groups. They talk about aiming to improve 'race relations' (in the third aim), presumably those between White and ethnically diverse groups. The fact that this document sets out the organisation's aims suggests that it could be a manifesto of some kind, or perhaps a promotional flyer or even a letter-head. Why it is held in a Colonial Office file is less clear; maybe it relates to the organisation and the promotion of its material in one of Britain's colonies at the time.

Why does The National Archives have this source?

This document is held within a Colonial Office file entitled 'St. Vincent: The Protest by the Coloured Peoples League against censorship'.

What is the context of this source?

The 1920s onwards saw an increase in racial awareness and unrest, for example the post-First World War race riots and the Special Restriction (Coloured Alien Seamen) Order of 1925. This growing awareness resulted in a developing understanding of Black British civil rights and the presence of organisations fighting for racial equality in Britain and the British Empire.

The League of Coloured Peoples (LCP) was founded in London by Jamaican-born Harold Moody. It focused on the promotion and achievement of Black rights in Britain. It published a civil rights journal *The Keys* from 1933 onwards, and its four main objects or aims were published in every edition. In 1937, LCP added a fifth objective, reflecting the economic hardship experienced by this community in the face of the 'colour bar': 'To render such financial assistance to coloured people in distress as lies within our capacity'.

Many Black people in Britain at this time were discriminated against due to their skin colour, for example, they were refused employment, housing and service in restaurants.

💡 LESSON IDEAS

ENQUIRY QUESTION
What does this document reveal about racial awareness in 1930s Britain?

Getting started

Use this document as part of your work to introduce students to post-First World War Britain, race relations and awareness of Black British civil rights at this time.

You might want to teach this lesson following Lesson 26 on the race riots in 1919. If so, begin with a short retrieval activity to assess what students can remember from this first lesson. If they need a reminder of the key facts about these riots, you could show them the short video produced by the Black Curriculum at **www.youtube.com/watch?v=AQ2HmVsQCIo**.

Exploring further

Ask students to read the document carefully and write down a few initial observations in response to these questions:

- What type of document do you think it is? Why?
- What appears to be important to the organisation it describes?

Now explore with the students why there was a need for organisations like The League of Coloured Peoples in the early 1930s. Why do the students think these organisations might have existed? What had been happening across Britain after the First World War and around this time with regards to race relations?

Introduce students to the fifth aim of The League of Coloured Peoples, added in 1937: 'To render such financial assistance to coloured people in distress as lies within our capacity.'

Why might this additional aim have been added in 1937?

Once you have drawn some conclusions to the questions being posed, set the students a short written task that asks them to summarise what the source reveals about race relations in Britain at this time.

Finally, introduce students to other organisations fighting for racial equality at this time, for example, The Negro Welfare Association. For homework, what can they find out about its aims and key figures? How did it differ from The League of Coloured Peoples? What more can be learned from The Negro Welfare Association about race relations in Britain after the First World War?

Follow-up tasks
- Students could investigate the life of Dr Harold Moody and how he came to establish The League of Coloured Peoples. Ask them to write a short argument for why Harold Moody should be remembered.

LESSON 32

INDIAN AIRMEN IN THE SECOND WORLD WAR

CONNECTION TO THE CURRICULUM

The Second World War and the wartime leadership of Winston Churchill

Aim: To find out about Indian airmen in the Second World War.

Historical event: Indian airmen in the Second World War

Source: A list of 'British Indian subjects serving in the Royal Air Force Voluntary Reserve' as Commissioned Officers (AIR 2/6876)

📖 TEACHER'S NOTES

What is this source?

This is a page from an Air Ministry and Ministry of Defence Registered File. It lists the names of 'British Indian subjects serving in the Royal Air Force Volunteer Reserve' as Commissioned Officers.

What can we infer from this source?

This document is a list of names predominantly typewritten, with a couple of handwritten annotations. The title tells us that these are the names of 'British Indian subjects serving in the Royal Air Force Voluntary Reserve' as Commissioned Officers. Many of the names are identifiable as Indian in origin. We can also infer that this is a record from the Second World War, as it was only after October 1939 that the RAF removed the colour bar, enabling people from across the Commonwealth, regardless of their nationality or race, to join the RAF.

Each person is listed by their RAF Service Number, followed by their rank (Pilot Officer, Flight Officer, etc.) and their name. Some of these men have additional information after their names that can reveal a little more about awards they may have been given, or whether they have been killed or are missing in action. We can see that a number of these men have been killed, or are presumed dead, reflecting how dangerous it was to serve in the RAF during the Second World War.

The ranks, and the fact that they were all Commissioned Officers, tell us that these men held some status and were of a higher rank within the RAF Voluntary Reserve. A number of them have also been awarded the Distinguished Flying Cross (D.F.C.), which was given for acts of courage while flying in operations against the enemy, suggesting skill and bravery.

Why does The National Archives have this source?

This document is held within an Air Ministry and Ministry of Defence Registered File and is dated 1943–44.

What is the context of this source?

The RAF Volunteer Reserve (RAFVR) was established in 1936, with the aim of providing a reserve of aircrew in the event of the outbreak of war. The Indian Air Force (IAF) was also established in 1928 (Indian volunteers had served as fighter pilots during the First World War). The IAF was open to men of all faiths and No. 1 Squadron was formed in 1933, officially entering the Second World War in September 1939.

In 1939 the RAF removed the colour bar, enabling people from across the Commonwealth of all nationalities to join. The following year, 24 Indians were sent to the UK for pilot training, eight of whom trained as fighter pilots and began flying in RAF squadrons. Around 200 Indians living in Britain also volunteered to join the RAF and Women's Auxiliary Air Force.

💡 LESSON IDEAS

ENQUIRY QUESTION
What does this document reveal about the RAFVR during the Second World War?

Getting started

Use this document to introduce students to the RAFVR and the role of Indian airmen during the Second World War.

Hide the title of the document and ask students to spend a couple of minutes scanning the document and writing down observations:

- What type of document do they think it is and why?
- What can they infer about the people and their ethnicity from the list of names?
- What jobs or roles are these people doing?
- Can they suggest a date for the document based on the above inferences?

Now reveal the title and explain the provenance of the document.

Exploring further

Ask the students what else they'd like to know about this document. Are there any abbreviations or terms that they've not seen before? What could these stand for and what do they reveal about some of the airmen in the list? Only give students the definitions of abbreviations after they've spent time discussing their own ideas.

Finally, facilitate a class discussion to answer the enquiry question.

Follow-up tasks

- Students can investigate the Indian men who served in the RAF or RAFVR during the Second World War, such as Pilot Officer Mahinder Singh Pujji, who flew Hurricanes.
- Introduce students to K.S. Nair's book *The Forgotten Few*.

LESSON 33

CARIBBEAN AIRMEN IN THE SECOND WORLD WAR

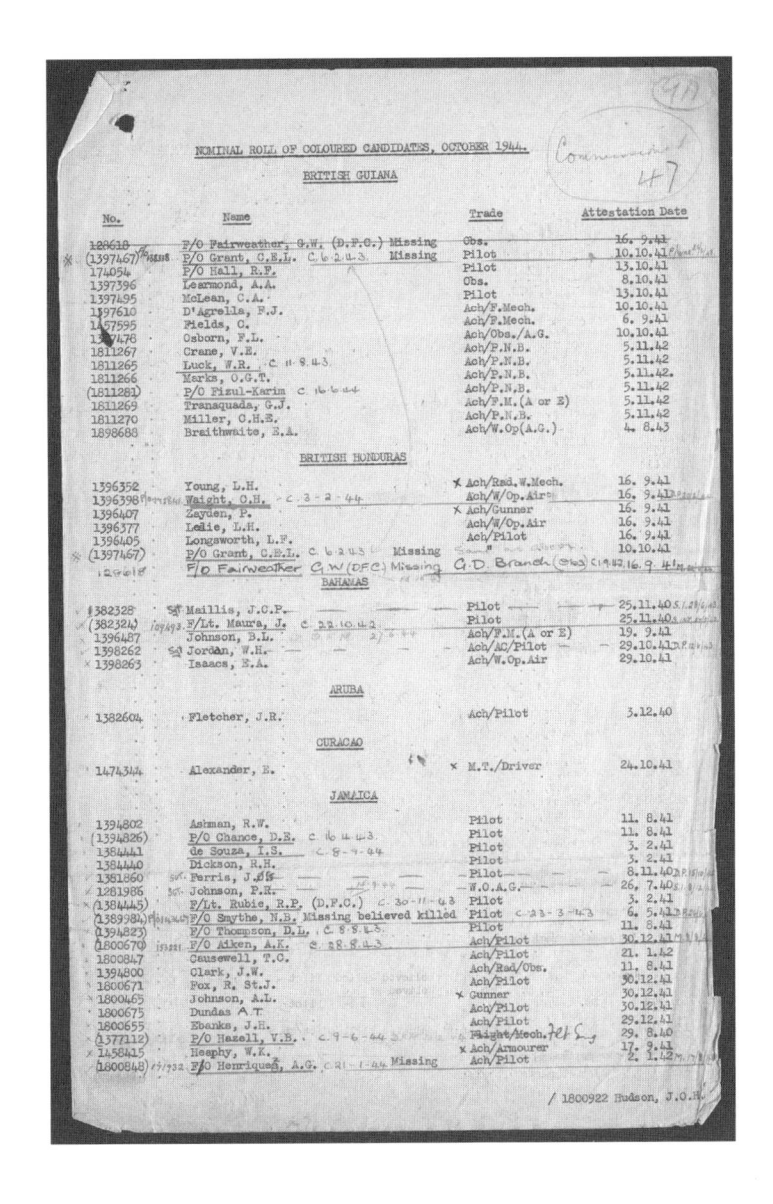

> **CONNECTION TO THE CURRICULUM**
> The Second World War and the wartime leadership of Winston Churchill
> **Aim:** To discover the Caribbean contribution in the Second World War.
> **Historical figures:** Dudley Thompson and others
> **Source:** Roll of candidates (AIR 2/6876)
> **Caution:** This source uses language that is inappropriate and unacceptable today.

TEACHER'S NOTES

What is this source?

Using language of the time, which is inappropriate today, this page entitled 'Nominal Roll of Coloured Candidates, October 1944' comes from a folder entitled 'Details of Commissioning, Decorations and Casualties of ~~Coloured~~ British Non-European Aircrew'. Note, the word 'Coloured' was crossed out on the original file.

What can we infer from this source?

We can infer from the document that colonial support for Britain was vital to the war effort both in the services and at home. The document is part of a longer list which shows the date that men enlisted into the Royal Air Force and their different roles. We see how the different countries of the Caribbean contributed: British Guiana (now Guyana), British Honduras (now Belize), the Bahamas and Jamaica. Aruba and Curaçao form the Caribbean part of the Kingdom of the Netherlands. The document also records the fate of certain personnel during the war.

'Attestation' is the process of swearing allegiance to the monarch and being formally accepted into her service, in this case the Royal Air Force. The document also contains many abbreviations relating to roles in the RAF:

Ach/F.Mech: Aircraft Hand/Flight Mechanic
Obs: Observer
W/Op: Wireless Operator
PNB: Pilot Navigational Bomber
AG: Air Gunner
MT: Mechanical (Motor) Transport
FM: Flight Mechanic

Why does The National Archives have this source?

The page comes from a file held by the Air Ministry, which we can tell from the reference.

What is the context?

It is hard to provide accurate statistics for the total number of Black men and women from Britain, the Caribbean and Africa who served in the war or on the home front. Records were not always kept and ethnicity not always listed. Therefore, this source from the Air Ministry showing the contribution of Caribbean airman is very unusual. A minute sheet in the file called 'Coloured personnel serving in the RAF' says that the number 'of personnel, coloured or believed to be coloured, entered in the RAF since 1940 for aircrew or ground duties is 618, 23 of who have been discharged'. Of that figure it points out that 103 have become officers (leaders of men) and 492 other ranks. Five have received 'Distinguished Flying Crosses and 3 Distinguished Flying Medals'. Finally, there are 173 ground personnel who are not commissioned officers.

This information was gathered, according to minutes in the file dated 12th May, 1945, to draw up a report on the contribution made by the colonial RAF personnel for a paper on the 'Recruitment of personnel from the colonies into the post-war Air Force'.

Diverse Histories © Clare Horrie and Rachel Hillman, 2022

💡 LESSON IDEAS

ENQUIRY QUESTION
What does this source reveal about the contribution of the Caribbean in the Second World War?

Getting started

Read over the source together and use questioning to ensure that students have understood the information in the source and its significance. You will likely need to define some of the terms and abbreviations, and also provide some context to the source.

The students can now write down five things they think the source reveals in relation to the enquiry question regarding the contribution of Caribbean men and women in the Second World War. They should also write down five questions they have about this topic that the source cannot answer.

Exploring further

Tell the students that they are now going to find out more about this topic by watching a short film. The film is called 'Hello West Indies' and it is available for free on the BFI Player at: **https://player.bfi.org.uk/free/film/watch-hello-west-indies-1943-online**.

This is a propaganda film from the British Ministry of Information, which shows servicemen and women from the Caribbean sharing messages with friends and family about the contributions they are making to the war effort. As they watch, ask the students to add to their notes in answer to the enquiry question. What more can this film tell them that the original source could not? Can they now answer any of the questions they wrote down during the starter activity? It's important to tell students that this is a propaganda film.

Ask them what they think this might mean about the information that it is providing. Is it a reliable source? Does it tell the whole story?

Using the students' notes from the original source and the film, begin to create a joint class slideshow or display about the contribution of Caribbean men and women in the armed services. Assign different groups, pairs or individuals a slide to contribute to the presentation or a written piece to display. Include maps, photographs and any primary evidence as appropriate.

This lesson can also be used as a starting point for exploring the role of Black men and women from Britain and from Africa during the Second World War. You can use Lesson 34 to learn more about the contribution of African soldiers, for example, or you might want to investigate the Royal West African Frontier Force and the King's African Rifles. As you broaden and deepen the students' understanding across these lessons, they can continue to add to the slideshow or display.

Follow-up tasks

- Visit the Imperial War Museum or explore their online resources on the Second World War. What information can students find about the contribution of Black men and women to add to the slideshow or display?
- Teachers or students can consult Stephen Bourne's book entitled *War to Windrush: Black Women in Britain 1939 to 1948* for fascinating case studies of Black women in the services, including Amelia King in the Women's Land Army, and Lilian Bader in the WAAF.

LESSON 34

AFRICAN SOLDIERS IN THE SECOND WORLD WAR

> **CONNECTION TO THE CURRICULUM**
> Challenges for Britain, Europe and the wider world: 1901 to the present day
> **Aim:** To find out about the role of African soldiers in the Second World War.
> **Historical event:** African soldiers in the Second World War
> **Source:** Painting of an African soldier (INF 3/1697)

TEACHER'S NOTES

What is this source?

This is an image contained in a Ministry of Information file. The Ministry of Information was the central government department responsible for propaganda and censorship during the Second World War. The source is the original artwork of a painting showing an African soldier.

What can we infer from this source?

We can tell that this man is in the military because of the way he is dressed. He is wearing the Khaki Drill uniform of the British forces, made of a light cotton material, and a broad-brimmed hat. This type of uniform was first worn as early as 1848 by the men of the British Indian Army Corps of Guides (made up of British Officers and enlisted Indian soldiers serving on the North-West Frontier). Over time, this uniform was eventually used throughout the British Military during combat in desert, very warm or tropical conditions.

This African man is dressed in British military uniform, which suggests that he is fighting as part of the British Empire in one of the Second World War campaigns. African troops served with the British Army in numerous places during the conflict, including the Horn of Africa, the Middle East, Italy and Burma.

Why does The National Archives have this source?

This document is held within a Ministry of Information file, dated 1939–1946 and entitled 'General War Pictures: Servicemen of the Commonwealth: African Soldier'. Britain needed the help of her empire to support the war effort, both in terms of people to fight, and the resources and materials that each country could provide. As the Ministry of Information was responsible for publicity, propaganda and the fostering of high morale, this picture could have been intended for use to promote the war effort and to encourage recruitment amongst African soldiers.

What is the context of this source?

Many colonies and former colonies provided Britain with men to fight during the Second World War. From 1939 onwards, more than one million African men were sent to serve in combatant and non-combatant roles, mostly fighting for Britain.

The conflict changed the mindsets of many African men, fostering a growing sense of awareness of their place in the world and the push for independence after the war. Those who survived to return home had been promised military medals and pensions by the British and other colonial powers. Very few men received these, but instead were faced with unemployment and continued colonial rule. The revolution for independence swept across Africa and by 1970 there were 45 African countries who had gained their independence.

💡 LESSON IDEAS

ENQUIRY QUESTION
What does this document reveal about the role of African soldiers in the Second World War?

Getting started

Use this document as part of your work to introduce students to African soldiers' contributions to the war effort.

Ask the students to look at the document carefully. What can they see in the image? What inferences can they make based on their observations? Who is this person? What role does he do? How can they tell?

Exploring further

Ask students to consider why this image was painted and what the Ministry of Information might have used it for. Who was the intended audience? Why do they think this? Now the students can brainstorm responses to the enquiry question: what does this document reveal about the role of African soldiers in the Second World War?

Introduce students to the 'All that's interesting' site at **allthatsinteresting.com**, which contains around 40 photographs relating to Africans serving in the Second World War. Show them a selection of photographs and allow the students to choose four images that interest them in particular. Display the photographs on the whiteboard. In pairs or groups, students can now select one of the photographs and use their inference skills to explore what further information their image reveals about African soldiers at this time.

Follow-up tasks

- Ask students to listen to the 30-minute audio documentary (or select extracts for them to listen to) by Martin Plaut, based on his original three radio programmes for the BBC World Service: **www.bbc.co.uk/worldservice/documentaries/2009/11/091112_fridaydoc_africasforgottensoldiers.shtml**.
- Can students produce their own short podcasts based on their research about African soldiers serving in the Second World War?
- Introduce students to *Fighting for Britain: African Soldiers in the Second World War* by Martin Plaut and David Killingray.

LESSON 35

GOLD COAST IN THE SECOND WORLD WAR

Your Manganese makes STEEL for fighting ships

Thank you Gold Coast!

CONNECTION TO THE CURRICULUM
Challenges for Britain, Europe and the wider world: 1901 to the present day
Aim: To find out about the role of the Gold Coast in the Second World War.
Historical event: Gold Coast in the Second World War
Source: Propaganda leaflet (INF 2/5)

TEACHER'S NOTES

What is this source?

This is a propaganda leaflet produced by the Ministry of Information during the Second World War.

What can we infer from this source?

We can see that this propaganda leaflet has been produced with a very specific audience in mind: people living and working on the Gold Coast. The illustration of the war ship fighting at sea and the reference to 'fighting ships' suggests this document was made during the Second World War; a time when the Gold Coast was a colony of the British Empire.

At the top of the leaflet, we can see an image of West Africans mining manganese. This is a brittle, silvery metal and was in great demand during both world wars. People are standing in the pit that has been carved into the mountainside, and some of them are carrying heavy loads on their heads. Machinery is being used to help mine the manganese and a steam train can be seen with carriages full of this precious cargo.

The caption reads 'Your Manganese makes STEEL for fighting ships. Thank you Gold Coast!' Britain is obviously keen to have the help of her colonies in the war effort, and this propaganda leaflet is endeavouring to gain support from the people of the Gold Coast. 'Your Manganese' implies that this resource is being offered willingly and downplays Britain's role as the country controlling this situation. The addition of the words 'Thank you Gold Coast!' further support this idea, as though the relationship between the two countries is a partnership and one of equality.

Why does The National Archives have this source?

This document is held within a Ministry of Information file. Britain needed the help of her colonies to support the war effort, and propaganda like this was used to gain support for these contributions.

What is the context of this source?

Many colonies and former colonies provided Britain with men to fight in the war, along with resources, all of which were crucial to the war effort. Germany and her allies worked to persuade people from the colonies of the British Empire to strive for their independence. They hoped to weaken Britain and damage the support it needed for the war effort.

The Gold Coast was vitally important to Britain for its strategic significance and also because of the resources it could provide. Thousands of men were recruited to fight, and natural materials such as manganese were mined to support the production of war equipment. The peacetime army of the Gold Coast increased to around 70,000 men during the Second World War. Those working in the mining industry saw limited wage increases, which were in no way comparable with the wages of European miners.

When those West African servicemen who had survived the conflict returned home at the end of the war, they were faced with unemployment and continued colonial rule. Their frustration was evident in riots against the lack of war pensions and jobs in Accra in 1948, which was the start of the push towards independence. The Gold Coast was the first African colony to gain its independence in March 1957, becoming the country of Ghana.

💡 LESSON IDEAS

ENQUIRY QUESTION
What does this document reveal about the role of the Gold Coast during the Second World War?

Getting started

Use this document to introduce students to the way in which colonies provided the British Empire with men and resources during the Second World War.

Give the students five minutes to study the leaflet and make a note of everything they can see. Once they have had two or three minutes to note down their initial observations, ask them to think in particular about how Britain is being portrayed in the leaflet. Why do they think this is?

Exploring further

Now ask the students to look again at the leaflet and answer the questions below. They could produce written responses to these questions or discuss them in pairs or groups and write notes.

- Why does the leaflet use both text and illustrations?
- How effective are the text and illustrations in conveying the message of the propaganda? Explain your reasoning.
- How does the leaflet use language in different ways to persuade the reader (for example, the use of personal pronouns 'you' or 'your'). How often are these used and why?
- What does the leaflet suggest about the relationship between Britain as a colonial power and the Gold Coast?

Using their responses to the questions, the students should now be able to draw some conclusions regarding the enquiry question: what does this document reveal about the role of the Gold Coast during the Second World War?

You can introduce students to further propaganda produced by Britain during the Second World War to influence West Africa on The National Archives website: **www.nationalarchives.gov.uk/education/resources/wartime-propaganda/**.

Follow-up tasks

- Ask students to explore the following websites that provide overviews of the role of West Africa in the Second World War:
    - **https://fpif.org/how_west_africa_helped_win_world_war_ii/**
    - **www.britishmilitaryhistory.co.uk/docs-e-w-s-africa-1930-1947-west-africa-1930-1947/**
- Go on to teach Lesson 47 to explore how the Gold Coast gained independence and became the country of Ghana in 1957. To what extent did the Second World War influence the push towards independence and what other factors were involved?

LESSON 36

NURSING IN THE SECOND WORLD WAR

CONNECTION TO THE CURRICULUM

The Second World War and the wartime leadership of Winston Churchill

Aim: To find out about the contribution of African nurses during the Second World War.

Historical figure: Princess Ademola

Source: Still from the film *Nurse Ademola* (Imperial War Museum item D16164). ©Imperial War Museum (D16164)

📖 TEACHER'S NOTES

What is this source?

The Colonial Film Unit made a film during the war called *Nurse Ademola*, aimed at maintaining the support of the colonies in the British Empire. Unfortunately, a copy of the film no longer exists today, but this source is a still from the film. The caption of this photograph is: 'After her training is completed "Nurse Ademola" starts her long journey home. Two of her friends from the hospital come to see her off.'

What can we infer from this source?

The photograph was produced by the Ministry of Information division of photographs. It comes from the propaganda film of the life of Nurse Ademola, which showcased her work but was also used to garner support from Britain's colonial allies.

Princess Omo-Oba Adenrele Ademola was the daughter of the Alake of Abeokuta, a significant king in the southern region of Nigeria. Princess Ademola attended school in Somerset in 1936, after which she began a life and career in British nursing that spanned over 30 years. For Britain, Princess Ademola was a nursing role model not only for Africans but also for the British Empire.

We can infer from the photograph that Princess Ademola was quite privileged: she is well dressed and seems to be travelling first class. There are no other women of colour at the station seeing her off. Perhaps it was unusual for women from the colonies to have sufficient wealth to train as nurses in Britain?

Why does the Imperial War Museum hold this source?

This is a photograph held at the Imperial War Museum photographic archive, but it is a Ministry of Information government document. It is part of the Ministry of Information for the Second World War official collection.

What is the context of this source?

Adenrele Ademola was a Nigerian princess and nurse. She trained in London in the 1930s and worked in the capital during the Second World War. She was the daughter of the Alake of Abeokuta, a king from the southern region of Nigeria. Princess Ademola was educated in Somerset and trained as a nurse at Guy's Hospital in London, qualifying as a registered nurse in 1941. She worked at Queen Charlotte's Maternity Hospital in London and New End Hospital in Hampstead in 1942. After the war, many women from Commonwealth countries came to train and work as nurses in hospitals as part of the new National Health Service (NHS).

💡 LESSON IDEAS

ENQUIRY QUESTION
What role did African nurses play during the Second World War?

Getting started

This photograph highlights the role played by women during the Second World War, but specifically gives insight into the contribution made by African nurses. In the broader context, it is important to discuss with students that the contribution of Black women in the services and on the home front has often proved absent from many history books about the Second World War. Facilitate a brief class discussion to explore the following questions:

- Why is this the case?
- Are things changing?

Exploring further

Carefully examine the photograph. Divide the pupils into groups to consider one of the following questions so they can report back as 'the class expert' for their question:

- What does the photograph show?
- How can we date it?
- What can you infer from this photograph?
- Why do you think this photograph was taken?
- Who is the possible intended audience?
- What do you think was the significance of Princess Ademola's career for nursing in Britain at this time?
- How useful is this source for historians researching the Second World War?

Hand out copies of the following blog post about Princess Ademola: **https://blog.nationalarchives.gov.uk/african-princess-in-guys-the-story-of-princess-adenrele-ademola/**.

Can the students now create a profile of Princess Ademola and write a short persuasive speech about why she should appear in the history books about the Second World War?

Follow-up tasks

- Explore further the role of Black women during the Second World War with *West Indian Women at War* by Ben Bousquet and Colin Douglas. This book describes the contribution made by West Indian Women in the British Armed forces and the reluctance of the British War Office to recruit them. Women were first recruited from the Caribbean in 1943 into the Auxiliary Territorial Service.
- Stephen Bourne has documented the role of Black women in Britain from 1939 to 1948 in his book *War to Windrush*. The book includes a huge number of photographs and interviews and provides important insight into the lives of these women. Teachers can share some of the stories in this book with students.
- Based on the students' additional research, create a classroom display on the contribution made by Black women during the Second World War.

LESSON 37

INDUSTRY IN INDIA IN THE SECOND WORLD WAR

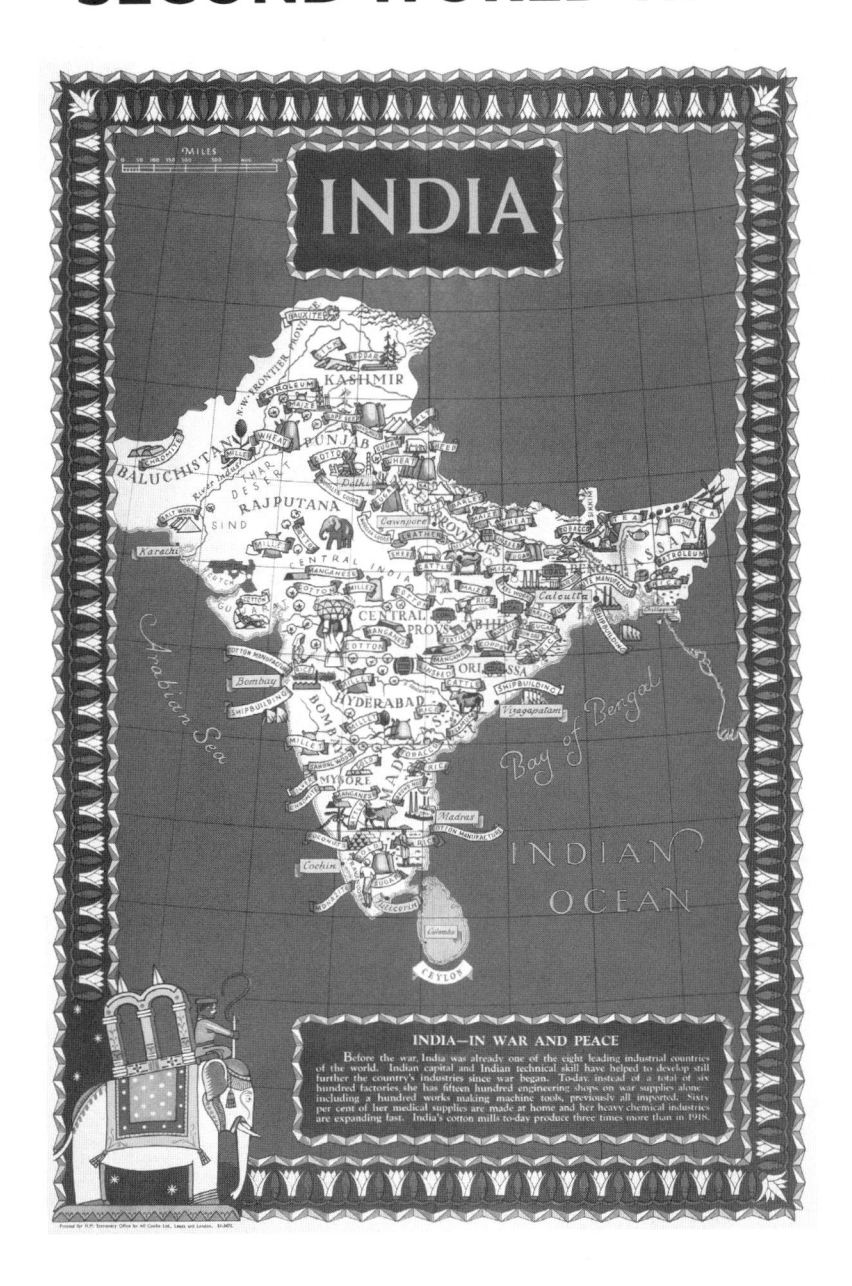

CONNECTION TO THE CURRICULUM
The Second World War and the wartime leadership of Winston Churchill
Aim: To find out about India's industry during the Second World War.
Historical event: India's contribution to the Second World War
Source: Illustrated map of India (INF 2/3)

TEACHER'S NOTES

What is this source?

This is an illustrated map of India taken from material held within the Ministry of Information (responsible for publicity and propaganda) and Central Office of Information files (responsible for marketing and communications).

What can we infer from this source?

This document is a beautifully illustrated map of India before Partition (evident by the presence of Kashmir), which can help us to date when it was created. The different regions of India have been labelled, along with key towns and rivers, and the map has been carefully illustrated with pictures of animals, landscapes, buildings and people. There is also information detailing the resources that are produced in each area, for example, petroleum and rice in Assam, and coal in Calcutta.

At the bottom of the map, there is a short paragraph entitled 'India – in War and Peace'. This describes how India was already 'one of the eight leading industrial countries of the world' before the outbreak of war. The writer goes on to explain that war has actually been of 'benefit' to India and her industries, enabling her to significantly increase the number of her factories. India is far less reliant on importing goods, such as machinery and medical supplies.

From the language used, we can infer that this document is designed to promote the positive impact of war on India and her people. It is focused on the industrial progress that has been made and how this economic upturn has made India a more powerful industrial player on the global stage. It acknowledges India's role in this – how her capital and technical skill have 'helped' to develop her industry – but implies that this would not have been possible without the impact of war. The document makes no reference to the tragedy of war and the significant loss of life that Indian fighting forces were suffering.

Why does The National Archives have this source?

This document is held within the Ministry of Information and Central Office of Information files. It is dated 1943.

What is the context of this source?

India played a significant role in the Second World War and the fight to defeat the Axis Powers. Over 2.5 million Indians fought under British Command across the globe, including Indian airmen and naval personnel.

The war provided a boost to India's economy and industrialisation. Older industries such as cement, cotton textiles and sugar all expanded. Newer industries also sprung into production, making things such as diesel engines, machine tools and sewing machines.

The Second World War brought other changes. Different nationalities passed through the country, whilst thousands of Indians fought abroad. Society changed, allowing opportunities for work and social advancement. The construction of airfields and dockyards occurred at a rapid pace.

Rural economies suffered, as food was diverted towards the war effort and Indian fighting forces suffered a huge loss of life. For India, as for countries across the world, the war was a significant human tragedy.

💡 LESSON IDEAS

ENQUIRY QUESTION
What does this document reveal about India and her industries during the Second World War?

Getting started

Use this document to introduce students to the growth of India's industries during the Second World War.

Allow the students to look at the document for five seconds.

- What did they notice?
- What impressions do they have about the type of document this is and when it was created?

Now give them longer to study the document.

- What did they miss initially?
- How have their first impressions of the record changed now they've had an opportunity to study it for longer?

Exploring further

Once you have given students some context and further information regarding the source, invite them to explore it more critically. Use the following questions to prompt discussion in groups or as a class, before using responses and notes to draw conclusions in relation to the enquiry question:

- What impression does this document give about India and her industry during the Second World War?
- Why do you think the creators of the document wanted to portray the benefits of war on India and her people?
- Are there any other consequences of the war that might have been omitted from this document? Why have the creators omitted them?
- What other documents could the students look at to give them different interpretations of the impact of war on India and her people?

Follow-up tasks

- Introduce students to *Now or Never* by Bali Rai, a novel about a 15-year-old boy Fazal, from Rawalpindi in India, who lies about his age in order to enlist in the Royal Indian Army Service Corps. What can the students learn from this story about the impact of the war on the people of India?

LESSON 38

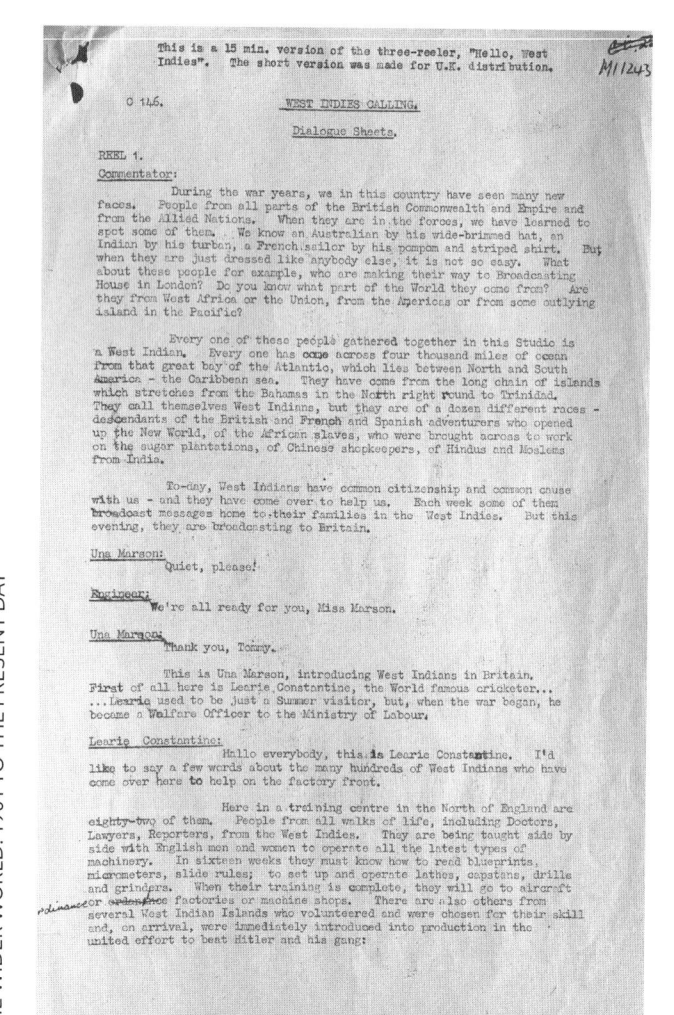

WEST INDIES CALLING

CONNECTION TO THE CURRICULUM

The Second World War and the wartime leadership of Winston Churchill
Aim: To explore the West Indies' contribution in the Second World War.
Historical figures: Una Marson, Learie Constantine and Ulric Cross
Source: Extracts from the production notes of *West Indies Calling* (INF 6/1328)

TEACHER'S NOTES

What is this source?

This source consists of extracts from the production notes for a 15-minute documentary film called *West Indies Calling*, made for the Ministry of Information by director Paul Rotha. The films showed how men and women from the West Indies were supporting Britain on the home front and in the military services.

What can we infer from this source?

A radio broadcast from the BBC in London to the West Indies is portrayed in the film. This was based on a show at the time named *Calling the West Indies*, produced by Una Marson for BBC Radio. Marson also appears in the film with cricketing star Learie Constantine and Ulric Cross, who describe the contribution made by West Indian people during the war. We can infer from the film Britain's desire to maintain the colonial support; this was vital to the war effort both at home and in the services. It also suggests a sense of unity and friendship between Britain and the West Indies as 'for the first time they try and understand each other and real friendship begins'.

Constantine explains that West Indians have come over to work in factories and machine shops with English workers and 'this will mean a lot during reconstruction after the war'. Ulric Cross, a flying officer from Trinidad, points out that there were West Indians in the Army, Navy and Air Force, and women in the WRENs, WAAF, ATS and nursing services working with others from the British Commonwealth of Nations.

Why was this film made? Perhaps to ensure and maintain support from the colonies of the British Empire during the war. It presents the idea of a people's war, which was familiar messaging in many propaganda films at the time. What is unusual is that it shows more diversity on the home front and within the armed services.

Why does The National Archives have this source?

The original production notes for the film are held in National Archives Ministry of Information collections. The film itself is also a public record, preserved and presented by the BFI National Archive on behalf of The National Archives.

What is the context of this source?

A longer version of the film was created in 1943 and called *Hello! West Indies*. Shockingly, at the same time, cricketer Learie Constantine was in London to take part in a match between an England eleven and an Empire eleven and was requested to leave the Imperial Hotel according to the 'colour bar'. He took the hotel to court and won his case, proving racial discrimination.

The film, while it recognises the contribution of the West Indies to the war effort, also acts as propaganda to maintain and create more support for Britain and the allies against the axis powers. Indeed, it is hard to provide fully accurate statistics for the number of Black men and women from Britain, the Caribbean and Africa who served in the war or on the home front. Records were infrequently kept and ethnicity not always listed.

LESSON IDEAS

ENQUIRY QUESTION
What does this source reveal about the West Indian contribution in the Second World War?

Getting started

Use this lesson as an introduction into the role played by the Caribbean in the Second World War. You can teach it alongside Lesson 33 on Caribbean airmen in the Second World War.

Read the source extracts for the commentary of the film *West Indies Calling*. As a class, start brainstorming answers to the enquiry question based on what can be inferred from the text. Now invite the students to watch the short film on the BFI Player. It is available for free at: **https://player.bfi.org.uk/free/film/watch-hello-west-indies-1943-online**. Ask the students to write down what else they have learnt from watching the film itself in answer to the enquiry question.

Exploring further

The students can then engage in a variety of written and drama activities based on the source and the film. You can choose to use any or all of the following activities:

- Create your own labelled storyboard for the film using the source and the film.
- Role play an interview with the director Paul Rotha about the ideas behind his film. Here are some suggestions of the questions the interviewee might like to ask:
  - What is the message of your film?
  - How have you tried to get your message over in the film? Give us some examples of particular scenes.
  - Can you describe the style of the film?
  - What is the significance of the songs used in your film?
- Write a report on the advantages and disadvantages of using this film to find out about the West Indian contribution during the Second World War.

Follow-up tasks
- Write a profile of the Jamaican poet Una Marson, who has the part of compere in the film.
- Use an atlas or globe to find all the locations mentioned in the source.
- Teachers or students can consult Stephen Bourne's book entitled *The Motherland Calls on Britain's Black Servicemen and Women, 1939–1945* for more detailed context on the contribution of Black men and women during the Second World War.

LESSON 39

NOOR INAYAT KHAN

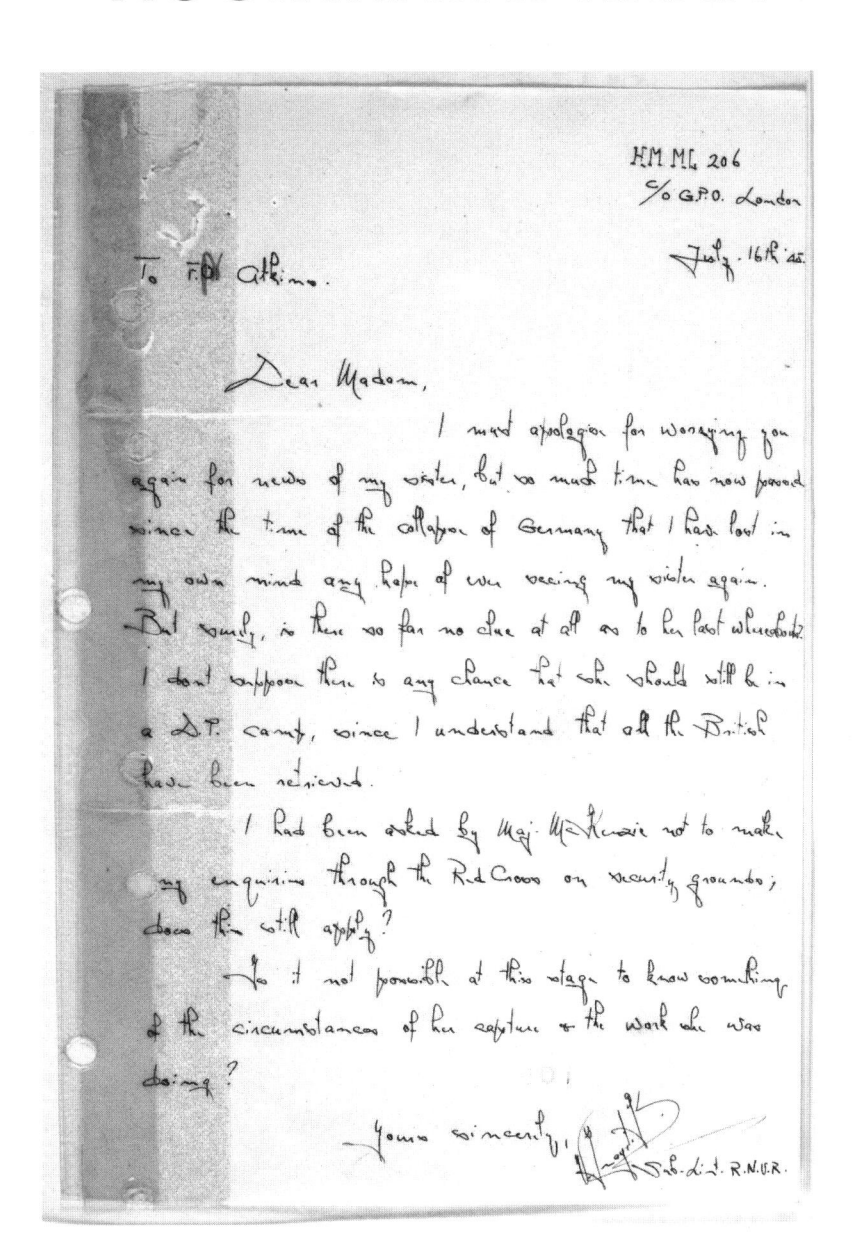

CONNECTION TO THE CURRICULUM

The Second World War and the wartime leadership of Winston Churchill

Aim: To explore the contributions of Noor Inayat Khan to the Second World War.

Historical figure: Noor Inayat Khan

Source: Request for information from Vilayat Khan on the whereabouts of his sister Noor Inayat Khan (HS 9/836/5 (105))

TEACHER'S NOTES

What is this source?

This source is a letter written by Vilayat Khan to Vera Atkins (a Special Operations Executive (SOE) intelligence officer who helped prepare SOE women for their missions). Vilayat wrote this letter in 1945, nine months after his family had found out that his sister, Noor Inayat Khan, was missing. Vera Atkins replied almost immediately and said that she was still waiting for news too, and that Vilayat could now make his own enquiries. It took a further two years for Noor's family to find out what had happened.

What can we infer from this source?

The author of this letter is very worried about his sister and it appears that he has already enquired a number of times about her whereabouts. We can infer from the letter that his sister is possibly in Germany, following the end of the Second World War. We understand that she is a British citizen and that at some point she was held in a 'Displaced Persons Camp'. Her work sounds like it was potentially dangerous and quite secretive. Indeed, she was possibly playing a significant role in the war effort. We know that she has been captured at some point, but there is very little information about what has happened to her subsequently.

Why does The National Archives have this source?

This letter comes from the personnel files of the SOE during the Second World War. It was closed until 2003 and the contents of this file were kept secret until this point.

What is the context?

Noor Inayat Khan was a British secret agent for the SOE during the Second World War. She was the first female wireless operator to be sent out to help the resistance movement in France. The resistance was made up of groups who were against Nazi rule and their occupation of France.

Noor helped the resistance by receiving and sending secret messages back to London. She was eventually captured by the Nazis, and for many months her family did not know what had happened to her. Noor Inayat Khan was executed in a concentration camp in 1944 and her last word before she died was *liberté*, meaning freedom. For her outstanding bravery, she was awarded the George Cross after her death.

💡 LESSON IDEAS

ENQUIRY QUESTION
What does this source reveal about Noor Khan and how she contributed to the Allied cause during the Second World War?

Getting started

Use this letter to introduce the work of Noor Inayat Khan as an SOE Operative. Noor is one of many brave recruits to the SOE, and students could also go on to explore other agents such as Christine Granville.

Ask students to brainstorm their own questions about the letter and then discuss their answers as a group. For example:

- What type of source is this?
- Who is the author writing to?
- Why did the author write this letter?
- What type of work do you think the author's sister did? Explain why you think this.

Exploring further

Now the students have some understanding of the role of Noor Inayat Khan, they can investigate the work of the SOE during the Second World War more generally by looking at some of the training materials available on The National Archives website. Choose some of the primary sources available at this link for the students to read and analyse: **www.nationalarchives.gov.uk/education/worldwar2/index-of-resources/western-europe/resistance**.

Follow-up tasks

- Find out about the work of other SOE agents at: **www.nationalarchives.gov.uk/spies/spies/default.htm**. The students can choose one SOE agent and create a zine-style fact file on their contribution to the Second World War.

LESSON 39
Noor Inayat Khan

TRANSCRIPT

HM ML 206
c/o GPO London

July 16th

To F.O. Atkins

Dear Madam,

I must apologise for worrying you again for news of my sister, but so much time has now passed since the time of the collapse of Germany that I have lost in my own mind any hope of ever seeing my sister again.

But surely, is there so far no clue at all as to her whereabouts? I don't suppose there is any chance that she should still be in a D.P. [Displaced Persons] camp, since I understand that all British have been retrieved.

I had been asked by Major McKenzie not to make any enquiries through the Red Cross on security grounds; does this still apply?

Is it not possible at this stage to know something of the circumstances of her capture and the work she was doing?

Yours sincerely,
Vilayat

LESSON 40

RACIAL DISCRIMINATION IN THE SECOND WORLD WAR

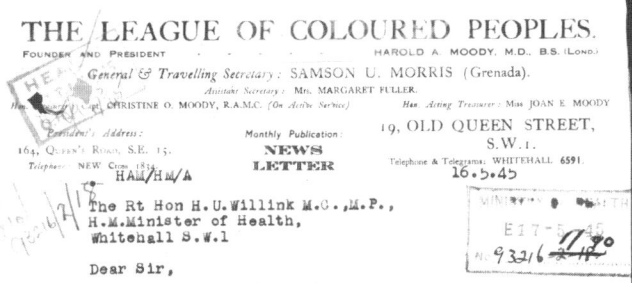

> **THE LEAGUE OF COLOURED PEOPLES.**
> FOUNDER AND PRESIDENT — HAROLD A. MOODY, M.D., B.S. (Lond.)
> General & Travelling Secretary: SAMSON U. MORRIS (Grenada).
> Assistant Secretary: Mrs. MARGARET FULLER.
> CHRISTINE O. MOODY, R.A.M.C. (On Active Service)   Hon. Acting Treasurer: Miss JOAN E. MOODY
> President's address: Monthly Publication   19, OLD QUEEN STREET,
> 164, Queen's Road, S.E. 15.   NEWS   S.W.1.
> Telephone: NEW Cross 1813   LETTER   Telephone & Telegrams: WHITEHALL 6591.
>
> HAM/HM/A   16.5.45
>
> The Rt Hon H.U.Willink M.C.,M.P.,
> H.M.Minister of Health,
> Whitehall S.W.1
>
> Dear Sir,
>
> I have been instructed to draw your attention to the fact that as a direct result of war conditions there are now emerging a large number of unwanted babies, of which a fair proportion are coloured. Agencies at present at work seem to be able to deal with the white babies, but are either unable or unwilling to deal with the coloured ones. Herein we detect the grave possibilities of an aggravation of the Colour Bar, just at a time when so much is being done to help to abolish this curse.
>
> In our experience the best way in which to deal with such a situation is by some wise action taken by an authoritative person; and we would venture to suggest that inthis case that person should be yourself.
>
> Our Organisation is opposed to the establishing of a Home for coloured babies as such, but we do feel that a Home should be established for these unwanted babies and that they should be admitted thereto in equal proportion of black and white.
>
> One of our members feeling the need for some action tried to establish such a home, but is finding this not so easy as he anticipated. We have had other suggestions and offers made to us from time to time, as to how to deal with this issue, but we do feel that it is a matter for
>   Government/
>
> Government action and that such action should be taken almost immediately, if we are to anticipate what might develop into a serious and perhaps awkward issue.
>
> We have no doubt, Sir, that your Department has had their attention drawn to this need, but we would like to have your assurance that you feel that you ought to do something about it; and that, in so doing, you will not ignore the help we are able to give in a matter of vital concern to us both as coloured people and as citizens of a country we love and whose good name we desire to see enriched.
>
> Yours very truly,
>
> Harold A. Moody,
> Founder & President

CONNECTION TO THE CURRICULUM

The Second World War and the wartime leadership of Winston Churchill

Aim: To explore issues of racial prejudice in wartime Britain.

Historical figure: Harold Moody, 1882–1947

Source: Letter from Harold Moody (MH 55/1656)

Caution: This source contains language that is inappropriate and unacceptable today.

TEACHER'S NOTES

What is this source?

This letter is from Harold Moody, founder of the League of Coloured Peoples, to the wartime Minister of Health.

What can we infer from this source?

Moody describes a serious problem of racial discrimination, as there is a 'large number of unwanted babies, of which a fair proportion are coloured. Agencies at present at work seem to be able to deal with the white babies but are unable or unwilling to deal with the coloured ones'. The letter attributes the increased numbers of 'unwanted babies' as a 'direct result of wartime conditions'. However, he does not explain these conditions: the stationing of 130,000 African American GIs in Britain from 1942 onwards in preparation for Allied offensives against Germany.

The moderate tone of the letter throughout is interesting, as it reveals a lot about the nature of the organisation, its leadership and methods of campaigning.

Why does The National Archives have this source?

The letter comes from a file held by the Ministry of Health, explaining the 'MH' in the document reference.

What is the context?

Harold Moody was a Jamaican doctor who immigrated to Britain in 1904. He campaigned for racial equality and founded the League of Coloured Peoples in 1931, which produced a monthly newsletter even throughout the war. He worked as a doctor during the Blitz and later helped the community of London's New Cross when it was bombed in 1944. During the war, the league pushed for the rights of Black servicemen and women in the armed forces. In 1944 it held a conference in London and drew up a 'Charter for Coloured Peoples'.

The League of Coloured Peoples was an organisation which campaigned for civil rights, including the removal of the colour bar, or the active discrimination in the workplace, social settings or housing, against Black people and those who are racially minoritised. It aimed to protect the social, economic and political interests of its members and improve relations between the races. It also wanted to engage its members in the welfare of Black people across the globe. Members included the first President of Kenya, Jomo Kenyatta, Jamaican writer and feminist (and the first Black female producer at the BBC), Una Marson, and Trinidadian historian and journalist, C.L.R. James.

The file which contains this letter also includes details of a conference about supporting illegitimate children during the Second World War. The League of Coloured Peoples and the National Council for the Unmarried Mother and her Child attended, along with other groups.

💡 LESSON IDEAS

ENQUIRY QUESTION
What does this letter reveal about racial discrimination during the Second World War?

Getting started

Teachers will need to handle this source sensitively. It is important to discuss with the students the attitudes towards interracial relationships today, prior to working with this document. Does the source reveal that attitudes have changed since the 1940s?

Exploring further

Present the source to the students and ask them to carefully examine the physical appearance of the source and its layout, then read it. The students should then create a presentation about the source in order to answer the enquiry question.

Explain to the students that they will need to create their own labels, questions and notes for their presentation. Here are some points or questions they could include:

- Comment on the type of source this is.
- Comment on the date or significance of when it was produced.
- Why has the source got stamps on it?
- Who are the people mentioned in the source?
- Explain why the letter was written.
- What does the term 'colour bar' mean? If you don't know, can you find out?
- Why do you think the number of babies of dual heritage increased at this time?
- Explain the work of the League for Coloured Peoples (LCP).
- Explain how the LCP was organised and how it spread its ideas. (The top of the source gives some clues.)
- Describe the tone and attitude of the letter. Clue: check out the final words.
- What other sources would help us to find out more about the LCP and its work?

Follow-up tasks

- Write a biography of the life of Harold Moody. Start by researching and creating a timeline of his life.
- Design a book cover for the biography of Harold Moody based on the timeline you have written.
- Consult resources on the Imperial War Museum website on Black GIs in Britain during the Second World War: **www.iwm.org.uk/history/they-treated-us-royally-the-experiences-of-black-americans-in-britain-during-the-second-world-war**.

LESSON 41

INDIAN SOLDIERS IN THE SECOND WORLD WAR

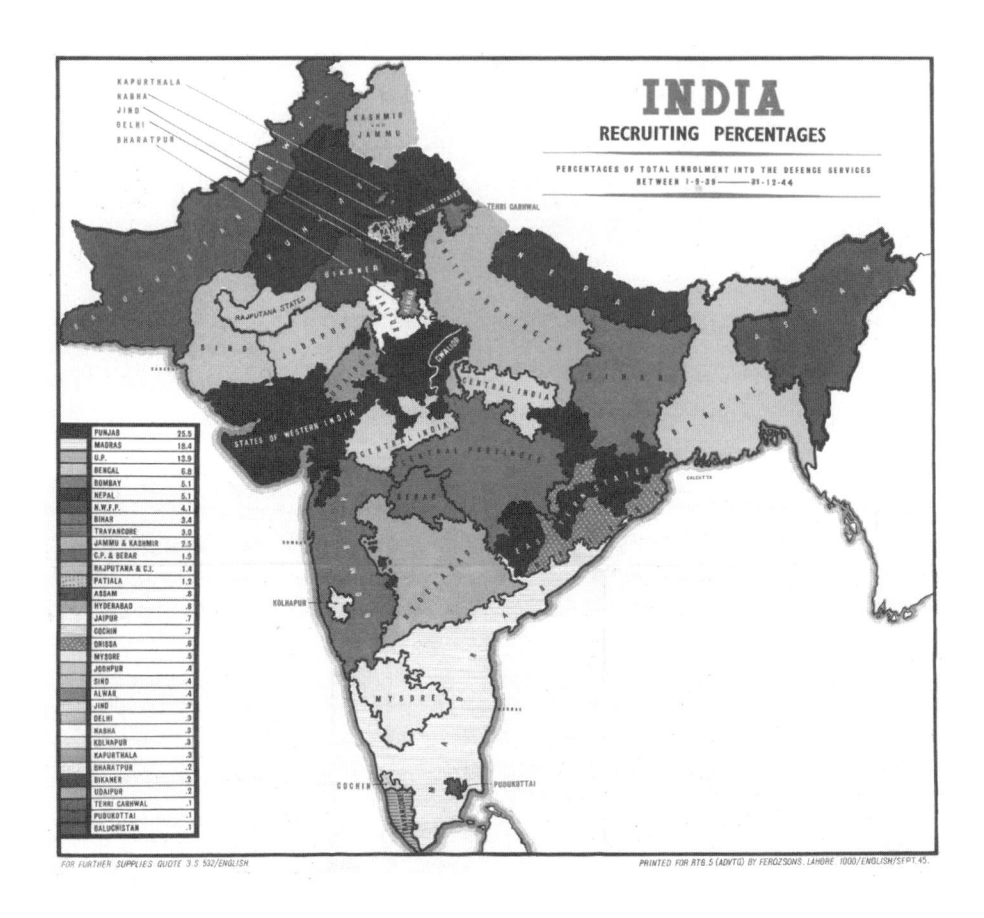

CONNECTION TO THE CURRICULUM

Challenges for Britain, Europe and the wider world: 1901 to the present day

Aim: To find out about Indian soldiers who fought during the Second World War.

Historical event: Indian soldiers in the Second World War

Source: Map of India (WO 32/14406)

📖 TEACHER'S NOTES

What is this source?

This is a map of India taken from War Office files. The War Office was a department of the British government that was in charge of the army.

What can we infer from this source?

We can see that this map was created before the Partition of India in 1947 (places such as Kashmir are shown; the Punjab region has not been divided into West and East). The document is dated 'Sept '45', and represents data gathered between 1939 and 1944.

Each region of India is illustrated with a different colour. There is a title and a key that provide further information about the colours and the percentages they relate to. We can quickly see that this map shows how many men from different parts of India were recruited into the 'defence services', (e.g. the army, the air force and the navy).

According to the document, the Punjab and Madras (now known as Chennai) regions recruited the highest numbers, whilst Pudukottai and Baluchistan had the smallest number of recruits. The size of the region doesn't seem to correlate with the number of recruits. For example, Baluchistan is a large area, whereas Bharatpur is much smaller in comparison, yet 0.2 per cent of its men were recruited (a higher percentage than that of Baluchistan).

Why does The National Archives have this source?

This document is held within the War Office files and is dated 1945.

What is the context of this source?

India played a significant role in the Second World War and Indian soldiers were recruited from different races and religions. Many soldiers were drawn from the Punjab. During the First World War over 500,000 Punjab soldiers were recruited to fight. Before that, the Punjab had displayed loyalty to the British during the Indian Uprising in 1857. By the end of the Second World War, the Indian Army numbered around 2,500,000 men, the largest volunteer army ever recruited. They fought across three continents, Europe, Asia and Africa, and over 4,000 medals were awarded to these soldiers.

Although the map is presumed just to count Indian men who were recruited into the defence forces, Indian women also played a significant role in the war. In 1942, the Women's Auxiliary Corps (India) (WAC(I)) was established and over 11,500 women had enlisted by the end of the war. These women fulfilled clerical and domestic duties. The WAC(I) also recruited women in its Air Wing, who operated switchboards and performed duties at air fields.

💡 LESSON IDEAS

ENQUIRY QUESTION
What does this document reveal about India and the recruitment of men into the 'defence services'?

Follow-up tasks
- Introduce students to Yasmin Khan's book, *The Raj at War*.

Getting started

Use this document to introduce students to the contribution made by Indian men to the defence services of Britain during the Second World War.

Allow the students to look at the document for five seconds:

- What did they notice?
- What type of document is this?

Now give them longer to study the document:

- What did they miss initially?
- How have their first impressions of the record changed?

Exploring further

Ask the students what information this document provides about India and the contribution of Indian men to the war effort. What other documents could the students look at to give them information about the impact of war on India and her people?

LESSON 42

THE PARTITION OF INDIA

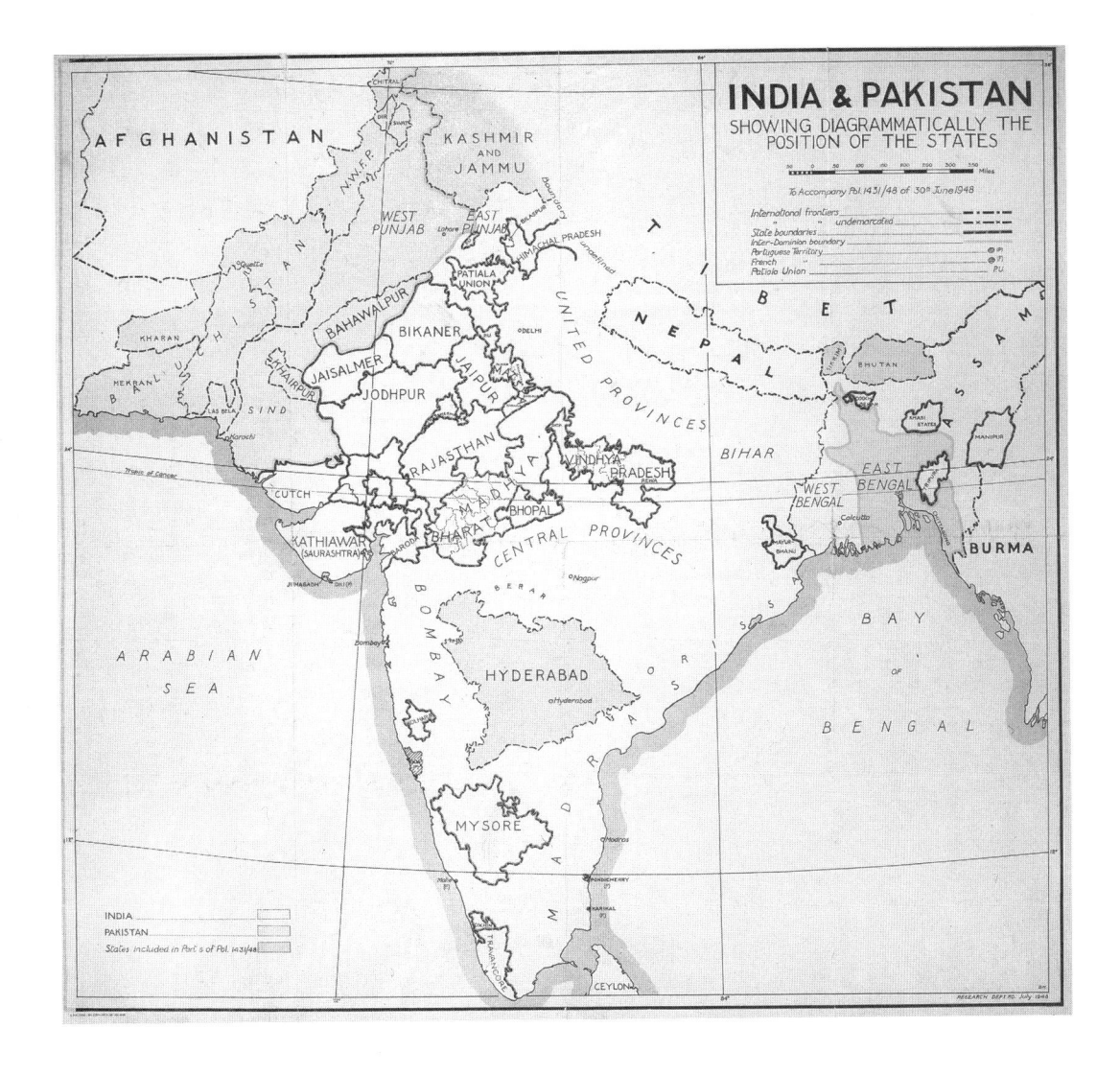

CONNECTION TO THE CURRICULUM
Challenges for Britain, Europe and the wider world: 1901 to the present day
Aim: To find out about the partition of India after the Second World War.
Historical event: Partition of India, 1947
Source: Map of India (MFQ 1/1145)

TEACHER'S NOTES

What is this source?
This is a map of India from a Foreign Office file. Dated 1948, it shows India and Pakistan following the partition of India in 1947.

What can we infer from this source?
We can tell that this map has been created after Partition in 1947. The map shows places where states were partitioned into either India or Pakistan at a slightly *later* date. For example, Kashmir, originally deciding to be independent from both Pakistan and India, chose to join India in October 1947. Conflict ensued and even today it is a contested area, with parts being recognised internationally as 'Indian-administered Kashmir' and 'Pakistan-administered Kashmir'. Bhutan and Sikkim were also not acceded to either India or Pakistan in 1947. Bhutan was recognised as independent from both countries in 1949, whereas Sikkim joined India in 1975.

This map shows the way in which India had been partitioned by 1948, and the areas that were still 'undecided'. However, it does not reveal the process that led to partition, nor the accounts of separated families; the human cost of dividing India in this way.

Why does The National Archives have this source?
This document was originally held within a Foreign Office file.

What is the context of this source?
Before India had begun to be colonised by European states in the sixteenth century, it had been a country of regional kingdoms, each ruled by Princely states.

By the nineteenth century, the voice of Indian people for independence from Britain grew louder. After the Second World War, Britain moved towards preparations for the transfer of power from the Raj to India.

There were differing political views amongst Indian leaders. Gandhi and Nehru, representing the Hindus, wanted one united India. However, Jinnah, representing the Muslims, advocated for a two-nation division of India, with Pakistan as a home for Muslims.

In a period of just five weeks, following Lord Mountbatten's short consultation with Indian ministers, politicians and his own staff, it was decided that Partition was the only solution.

Plan Balkan, the first draft of the plan for Partition, was met with strong criticism from Nehru, so another plan was devised. The Boundary Commission, using outdated maps and census data, divided the three provinces under direct British rule (Bengal, Punjab and Assan) along the lines of religious majorities. If a Hindu-majority area bordered another Hindu area, then it became part of India. But if a Hindu-majority area bordered a Muslim-majority area, then it could become part of Pakistan. Muslims and Hindus began moving to areas they thought would be their religious majority; they left their homes, their livelihoods and their relatives. Around ten million people tried to change lands in the summer of 1947 and only nine million made it to their new land. Over one million Indians were killed in the bloodshed that occurred.

The new map of India and Pakistan was revealed on 17th August 1947, but the ramifications of Partition had begun much earlier and continued long after.

Diverse Histories © Clare Horrie and Rachel Hillman, 2022

💡 LESSON IDEAS

ENQUIRY QUESTION
What does this document reveal about the Partition of India?

Getting started

Use this document as part of a series of lessons about the Partition of India.

Cover the main title of the source and ask the students to study the map carefully. Can they date the map? Why have they chosen this date? What do they think the different colour-coded areas reveal?

Exploring further

You should now explain to students what happened during the Partition of India, using the facts from the teacher's notes. What does this source reveal about the Partition of India and what is not revealed? Think about the terrible human cost of Partition and the role of Britain.

Ask the students what other documents historians could look at to give them an idea of what Partition was like for some of the people involved. Discuss their answers and then go on to explain that it is possible to listen to the lived experiences of some of those who survived Partition. As a class, you can then listen to and discuss some of the 10,000 oral histories in the 1947 Partition Archive: **www.1947partitionarchive.org**.

Follow-up tasks

- Introduce students to Yasmin Khan's book *The Great Partition*.
- Students could take a virtual tour of the Partition Museum in Amritsar, India, by exploring some of the resources available at **www.partitionmuseum.org**. Alternatively, they could look at the series of images of Partition from American photographer Margaret Bourke-White: **https://tribune.com.pk/story/864867/11-devastating-pictures-from-the-1947-partition**.
- Ask students to read *A Beautiful Lie* by Irfan Master, a novel about 13-year-old Bilal, a Muslim boy in India, who devises a plan with his friends to keep the news of Partition and the accompanying violence from his dying father.

LESSON 43

THE EMPIRE WINDRUSH

> INWARD TELEGRAM
>
> Copy   TO THE SECRETARY OF STATE FOR THE COLONIES
>
> FROM JAMAICA (Acting Governor)
>
> D. 11th May, 1948.
> R. 11th May 1948   23.10 hrs.
>
> IMPORTANT.
>
> Not numbered
>
> Your telegram No.499 of 1947
>
> Jamaican Workers for the United Kingdom.
>
> I regret to inform you that more than 350 troop-deck passages by EMPIRE WINDRUSH - your telegram MAST 272 refers - have been booked by men who hope to find employment in the United Kingdom, and that it is likely that this number will be increased by another 100 before the vessel leaves. Most of them have no particular skill and few will have more than a few pounds on their arrival.
>
> 2.   Public announcements on the difficulty of obtaining work have not discouraged these bookings and only 40 persons have, so far, provided information such as was sent with my savingram No.801 of 3rd December, 1947. This is being sent by airmail and every effort is being made to secure similar information in respect of the remainder in order that it may reach you as long as possible before the vessel arrives in the United Kingdom.

CONNECTION TO THE CURRICULUM

Challenges for Britain, Europe and the wider world: 1901 to the present day

Aim: To examine the story of the *Empire Windrush* in migration history.

Historical figures: Acting Governor of Jamaica; Secretary of State for the Colonies in 1948

Source: Telegram from the acting Governor of Jamaica (HO 213/714)

📖 TEACHER'S NOTES

What is this source?

This is a telegram from the acting Governor of Jamaica, a British colony in the Caribbean, to the Secretary of State for the Colonies in Britain. It is held in the Home Office files and describes the departure of Jamaicans coming to live and work in Britain who travelled on the *Empire Windrush* ship.

What can we infer from this source?

We can infer from the source that there were approximately 450 Jamaican men, with few skills and little money, who wished to travel to Britain for employment. Perhaps this could be explained by the lack of opportunities in Jamaica at this time. The telegram suggests that the journey was going to be uncomfortable, especially for those who had open berth 'troop deck' accommodation on the ship. The telegram is part of a series of communications and reveals the attitude of colonial power to be one of negativity and regret. It suggests that the authorities in Jamaica have stressed that there are difficulties in finding work in Britain.

Why does The National Archives have this source?

This is a Home Office record, although this information was also held by the Colonial Office for the Secretary of State of the Colonies.

What is the context?

Information about the passengers on the *Empire Windrush* mentioned in this telegram was held by the Board of Trade. This collection includes the passenger lists for the *Empire Windrush*, which brought people from the Caribbean to the UK and docked in Tilbury on 21st June 1948.

Between 1947 and 1970, nearly half a million people left their homes in the Caribbean to live in Britain. In March 1947, the Ormonde set sail from Jamaica to Liverpool to bring people hoping for a better future. Later that year another ship, the *Almanzora*, set sail for Southampton. The *Empire Windrush* later docked at Tilbury on Thames on the 21st June 1948 with 1,027 passengers. The ship was at sea for 30 days, setting off from Trinidad on 20th May, picking up passengers at Jamaica, Tampico (Mexico), Havana (Cuba) and Bermuda. The majority were men, but some women and children travelled too. They had a wide range of skills and included carpenters, engineers and Royal Air Force servicemen. Other passengers were housewives or domestic workers.

These people were British citizens, with the right to enter and settle in Britain. Many were responding to the British government's call for workers in the transport system, postal service and health service. Britain needed workers to help rebuild the post-war economy. Many settled in London or moved to other cities.

It is important to point out that in 2018 the story broke that some of the families of the Windrush migrants, after having made such an important contribution to Britain for decades, had been deported, denied access to the National Health Service, benefits and pensions, and sacked from their jobs. The British government has been forced to apologise and offer compensation to anyone who suffered in this way.

💡 LESSON IDEAS

ENQUIRY QUESTION
What does this source reveal about the significance of the *Empire Windrush* in migration history?

Getting started

Use this source to introduce the history of Caribbean migration. Through your teaching of this topic, you should aim to answer the questions below. You can pose these questions to students at the start of the lesson to see what they know already.

- When, where and why did these Commonwealth citizens come to Britain?
- What contribution did they make?
- What was their experience on arrival and beyond?

Exploring further

Students become 'an expert' on the value of this source for the history of Caribbean migration. Here are some possible prompt questions they can explore to gain expertise:

- What type of source is this?
- How can we date this source?
- What are the weaknesses of telegrams as historical sources?
- What does this source reveal about the significance of the *Empire Windrush*?
- What does this source not tell us?

Follow on from this with Lesson 44 about Sam Beaver King.

Follow-up tasks

- Create a map to show the journey of the Empire Windrush to Britain.
- Prepare a presentation on the significance of the *Empire Windrush* in the history of migration.
- Read extracts from *Voices of the Windrush Generation* by David Matthews. This is a collection of stories from the men, women and children of the Windrush generation.
- Create your own collection of oral histories and interviews for a class 'exhibition' on the 'Windrush generation' and their contribution to Britain.

LESSON 44

SAM BEAVER KING

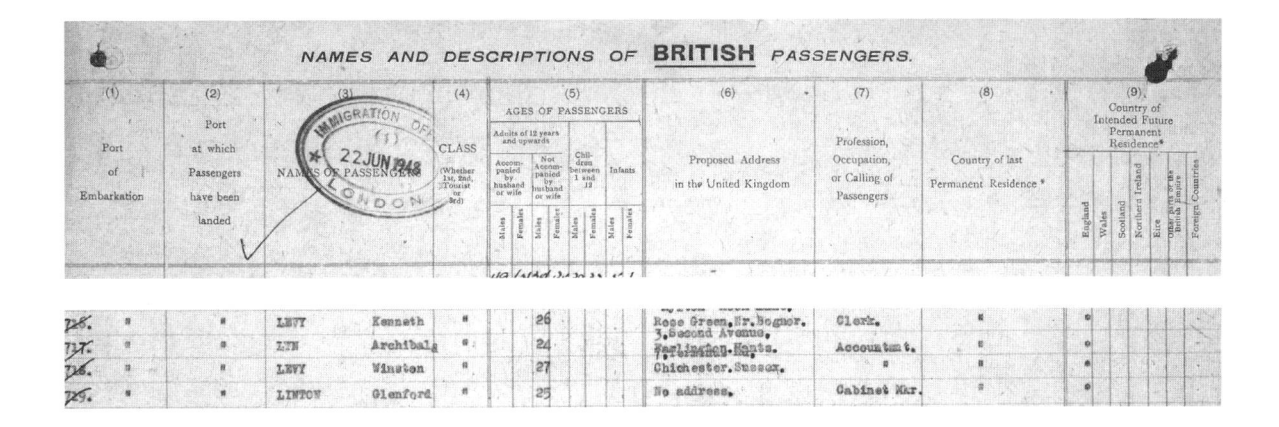

CONNECTION TO THE CURRICULUM

Challenges for Britain, Europe and the wider world: 1901 to the present day

Aim: To explore the impact of the 'Windrush generation'.

Historical figure: Sam Beaver King, 1926–2016

Source: Extract from the passenger list of the *Empire Windrush* (BT 26/1237)

TEACHER'S NOTES

What is this source?

This is an extract from one of the pages from the Board of Trade passenger list of the *Empire Windrush*, a ship which brought people from the Caribbean to the UK and docked in Tilbury on 21st June 1948.

What can we infer from this source?

The information given in these lists includes details about the passengers entering the United Kingdom by sea from ports outside Europe and the Mediterranean, including: port of embarkation and landing, age, occupation, address in the United Kingdom and the date of entering the country.

The source shows that Sam Beaver King came to Britain aged 22 on his own. His occupation in Jamaica was a carpenter and he planned to live in Nottingham. This source thus shows the start of his life in Britain. However, it does not reveal anything about what he went on to do or his significance in history. Did he change his occupation? Did he stay in Nottingham? What did he achieve?

Why does The National Archives have this source?

Passenger lists of people arriving in the United Kingdom by sea were kept by the Board of Trade's Commercial and Statistical Department. BT means Board of Trade in the document reference.

What is the context of this source?

Sam Beaver King, aged 22 years, arrived in Britain in June 1948 on the Empire Windrush. From Jamaica, he was a carpenter by trade. He had also served in the RAF during the Second World War.

King worked for the Post Office for 30 years. He went on to become the first Black Mayor of Southwark (in London) in 1983 and was co-founder of the first Caribbean carnival, a forerunner of London's Notting Hill Carnival. King also co-founded the Windrush Foundation in 1995 to help preserve the stories of the Windrush settlers. In 1998, he published his autobiography, *Climbing up the Rough Side of the Mountain*. All his life he worked to support the African-Caribbean community. He became a British citizen in 1966 under the British Nationality Act 1948. Sam Beaver King was awarded an MBE (Member of the Order of the British Empire) in 1998 as part of the 50th anniversary celebrations of Windrush Day.

The National Archives holds King's registration for British citizenship and those of the 380,000 Commonwealth immigrants who arrived in the UK between 1948 and 1971. The records give further insight about these citizens and complement the information found in the Board of Trade passenger lists.

Diverse Histories © Clare Horrie and Rachel Hillman, 2022

💡 LESSON IDEAS

ENQUIRY QUESTION
What does this source reveal about Sam Beaver King?

Getting started

Use this source to create a case study on the life Sam Beaver King to continue exploring the history of the 'Windrush generation'. Remember you are trying to answer the questions below in your teaching of the topic. You could use these questions as a quick retrieval task at the beginning of this lesson to assess what students learned (and can recall) from the previous lesson.

- When and why did these Commonwealth citizens come to Britain?
- What contribution did they make?
- What was their experience on arrival and beyond?

Exploring further

Facilitate a class discussion to answer the question: is this source *enough* to find out about Sam Beaver King and others like him who came to Britain? The students can discuss their answers as a group before coming together as a class to draw conclusions. Below are some questions to explore:

- What type of source is this?
- What does this source reveal about Sam Beaver King?
- What does it reveal about the other passengers?
- How can we date this source?
- What other sources would help us to find out more about Sam Beaver King?

To build the students' knowledge about Sam Beaver King and the experiences of those who travelled to Britain on the *Empire Windrush*, play students audio clips of Sam Beaver King describing his journey and arrival in Britain. You can also watch a Pathé video news clip with passenger interviews. These sources are all located here: **www.museumoflondon.org.uk/discover/how-did-empire-windrush-change-london-docklands**.

What more do these sources tell us about Sam Beaver King and the experiences of those who travelled on the *Empire Windrush*?

Follow-up tasks

- Produce a biographical leaflet on the significance of Sam Beaver King, including an image of his blue plaque (located in Warmington Avenue, London).
- Explore the Windrush Foundation website: **https://windrushfoundation.com**
- The class can produce an exhibition on the contribution made by migrants from the new Commonwealth countries to Britain. This could include, for example, their contributions to the NHS, British transport, art, music, literature, fashion and cuisine.

Diverse Histories © Clare Horrie and Rachel Hillman, 2022

LESSON 45

THE CAUSEWAY GREEN 'RIOTS'

> FOR the past eight months — since I arrived in Birmingham in search of a job — I have lived in the Causeway Green Hostel where the recent racial disturbances have occurred.
>
> The problem of Causeway Green is by no means unique in this country. It is an example of Great Britain's colour bar. Similar instances are constantly arising in other parts of the country.
>
> My 60 fellow West Indians in the hostel know only too well that the ill-feeling and fighting of the past week cannot be blamed on individual differences of opinion and local domestic arguments.
>
> The cause of the Polish-Jamaican dispute goes deeper than that. It is a result of cumulative ill-feeling and resentment, which has grown steadily for more than six months.
>
> Fundamentally it boils down to two main factors — accommodation and employment.

CONNECTION TO THE CURRICULUM
Challenges for Britain, Europe and the wider world: 1901 to the present day
Aim: To find out about race relations in post-war Britain.
Historical event: The Causeway Green 'Riots', 1949
Source: Extract from an article in the *Birmingham Gazette* (LAB 26/198)

TEACHER'S NOTES

What is this source?

This is an extract taken from a longer article published in the *Birmingham Gazette* on 10th August 1949. It has been kept within a Ministry of Labour and National Service file.

What can we infer from this source?

We can tell this document is an extract by the way it has been clipped from the larger source, and the style of print and font. It is written in the first person and the author is recounting their own experiences. They write that they arrived in Birmingham eight months ago seeking employment. They refer to their 'fellow West Indians' living in the Causeway Green Hostel where 'recent racial disturbances have occurred'.

The author believes that these incidents are not unique to the Causeway Green Hostel and are not the result of differences, but are due to 'Great Britain's Colour Bar', a social system where Black and other ethnic groups are not given the same opportunities and rights as White people. Inequality around accommodation and employment are at the heart of the issue. West Indians coming to Britain held British citizenship, whereas those under the European Voluntary Workers (EVW) scheme were deemed 'aliens', which meant that they could be kept within certain types of employment and their work was tightly controlled. This was breeding resentment.

Why does The National Archives have this source?

This document is held within a Ministry of Labour and National Service file. The government would have been monitoring these events.

What is the context of this source?

At the end of the Second World War, Britain faced a shortage of workers so looked to different sources for help. One of these was the EVW scheme; this helped those who had been made homeless and met demand for labour. At the same time, many people left their homes in the West Indies to live and work in Britain.

The Ministry of Labour and National Service set up the National Service Hostels Corporation (NSHC), which provided accommodation for the new migrants close to their places of work. Government files detail disturbances in many of these hostels across the country.

Staying at the Causeway Green Hostel in the West Midlands in August 1949, there were 235 Poles, 18 EVWs, 235 Southern Irish, 50 Northern Irish, 65 Jamaicans, and 100 English, Scottish and Welsh. There had already been earlier reports about disturbances between the Poles and the Jamaicans at Causeway Green. On Monday 8th August, a riot with serious fighting occurred. The following evening, the hostel sought to evict the Jamaicans (but not the Poles or others involved). The Jamaicans refused to leave.

Subsequently, the NSHC drew up a policy that discriminated further against Black men, limiting the number who could stay in each hostel.

It is worth noting that the Causeway Green Riots and events leading up to them mainly consisted of Polish men fighting an outnumbered group of Jamaicans.

💡 LESSON IDEAS

ENQUIRY QUESTION
What does this document reveal about feelings of racial inequality in post-war Britain?

Getting started

Use this document to introduce students to post-war Britain and race relations at this time.

Ask the students to read the extract.

- What does it tell us about the author's feelings about living and working in Britain?
- Why does the writer think that these racial tensions exist?

Exploring further

Using the teacher's notes, tell the students more about the context of the source and events at the Causeway Green Hostel. Ask them to think about the following questions:

- What does the subsequent action carried out by the NSHC following events at the Causeway Green Hostel reveal about racial prejudice in Britain at this time?
- What experiences do you think the Jamaicans and Poles had in common at this time?
- Why did these shared experiences not create a sense of unity amongst them?
- Do you think the NSHC would have reacted in the same way if the two groups of migrants had been White? Why/why not?
- When facing eviction, what do the actions of the Jamaicans involved reveal?

Follow-up tasks

- Introduce students to Kevin Searle's *'Mixing of the un-mixables': the 1949 Causeway Green 'riots' in Birmingham*, on whose research this lesson is based.
- Introduce students to the work of Charlie Brinkhurst-Cuff, *Mother Country: Real Stories of the Windrush Children*.

LESSON 46

'A WEST INDIAN IN ENGLAND'

Queueing

One of the first things I noticed reflecting on this was the queue. The idea of a queue is not English, but it has developed into a characteristic English institution. People queue for everything. They line up and patiently wait their turn for service. This enables those serving to deal with a tremendous number of people in a comparatively short space of time with a minimum of fuss and bother.

It would have done you good to see, for instance, the way the crowd was handled at the Olympic Games. Some eighty thousand people were sent home every evening in half an hour by the Underground and bus without the general transport system of London so much as turning a hair. Each morning the buses and tubes and trains take some three million people to their work in London in the space of an hour. That is more people than there are in the whole of the West Indies.

There is no "bumping and boring" to get into the cinema or to catch the bus after work. People queue quietly and take their turn. The conductors do not get hot and flustered or start to swear at the passengers.

14

and your people. The average English person knows nothing of the Colonies, and what is more he is not even curious. His picture, if he has one, is one that divides sharply the Dominions like Canada and Australia, where the people are much like himself and play a good game of cricket, from the Colonies which are inhabited by "natives", who wear very few clothes, do very little work, vary from the noble savage to petulant children, and speak an amusing variant of pidgin-English. This picture he gets from the children's "comics", the cheap novelette and the American moving pictures. He cannot be blamed for this, but the picture will annoy the West Indian who is apt to think of England as the "mother country".

have an additional difficulty, "colour prejudice". You may find that on answering an advertisement for lodgings by telephone or letter and saying you are a student or tourist you will be told by the landlady that the rooms are available, that the rent is so much, and would you like to come and have a look at them? On arrival, the landlady, suppressing a gasp, and puzzling over the fact that a coloured person could have so English a name as Smith or Brown, will politely tell you that she is very sorry, but that she has just let the rooms to someone else who also answered the advertisement. This will hurt, because in most cases you will be sure that it is untrue, but there is little that you or anyone can do about it. The basic cause is the misconception behind the prejudice. Often the landlady might have been prepared "to risk the unknown", but fear of what the neighbours would say has deterred her.

CONNECTION TO THE CURRICULUM

Challenges for Britain, Europe and the wider world: 1901 to the present day

Aim: To explore life in Britain for the early 'Windrush generation'.

Historical figures: Dudley Joseph Thompson and Hugh D. Carberry

Source: Pamphlet from 1949 called 'A West Indian in England' (CO 875/59/1, pages 14, 16, 18)

Caution: This source contains language that is inappropriate and unacceptable today.

TEACHER'S NOTES

What is this source?

These extracts come from a pamphlet from 1949 called 'A West Indian in England' from a file named 'Publications: Proposed Race Relations Pamphlet' belonging to the Colonial Office. It was written by H. D. Carberry and Dudley Thompson who 'attempted to give the visitor from the West Indies a fair and frank picture. . . of the circumstances he will find on his arrival in this country'.

What can we infer from this source?

Extract A concerns 'Queuing' and we can infer how Britain was supposed to be viewed by members of the colonies. It presents the idea that the British are very orderly and polite and queue for everything. The extract refers to the Olympics, which took place in London in 1948.

Extract B explores how the British might view people from the Caribbean and suggests that their opinions were based on racist stereotypes. The term 'mother country' is important here because many immigrants hoped that the 'mother country' would look after them and understand their Britishness.

Extract C explores the problems faced by some immigrants in finding accommodation when they arrived in Britain. It reveals racial prejudice and its personal impact. The extract also touches on the possible causes of prejudice as 'fear of the unknown' or 'what the neighbours would say'.

Why does The National Archives have this source?

The Colonial Office holds this pamphlet. The authors, both Jamaican immigrants and law students at Oxford, were asked by the Central Office of Information in 1949 to write a pamphlet to explain to anyone considering immigration to Britain what they could expect to find when they arrived.

What is the context?

Thompson had served in the Royal Air Force from 1941 to 1947 and Carberry was a poet and had been a civil servant in Jamaica. The Colonial Office in the Caribbean initially ordered 10,000 copies of the pamphlet.

The pamphlet includes a poetic description of the approach to London, where the authors observe that the light is never so 'fierce in intensity' nor the range of natural colours 'as great' as back home. It reveals the austerity of post-war Britain, and London is described as scarred by the effects of the Blitz. There are sections on 'the English reserve', the 'English climate and its functions', 'identity cards and ration books', 'good plain English cooking', 'restaurants', 'the Health Scheme', 'queuing', 'getting somewhere to live and the colour problem', 'Hyde Park', 'the English pub', 'students', 'workers', 'some hints to workers coming to England' and 'visitors'. This last section describes the tourist sights and the cities of Manchester, Liverpool and Cardiff. It says they have large immigrant populations 'descended of the original settlers from West Africa and West Indies'. These settlers were regarded as 'a social problem'.

The pamphlet was produced at an important time in the history of Caribbean immigration to Britain. In 1948, the Nationality Act was passed, meaning citizens of the colonies became British subjects with the right to live in Britain. By 1962, the Commonwealth Immigrants Bill restricted the entry of Commonwealth citizens into Britain.

💡 LESSON IDEAS

ENQUIRY QUESTION
What does this source reveal about life in Britain for immigrants after the Second World War?

Getting started

Use these pamphlet extracts to explore what life was like in Britain for Caribbean immigrants after the Second World War. This lesson can be used in conjunction with Lessons 43 and 44 in this book based on the Windrush generation and Sam King.

Divide your students up into small groups to explore a different extract. Explain the context of the source and ask them to feed back what their extract suggests about life in Britain for immigrants after the Second World War.

You could use these questions to prompt the discussion:

- What type of source is this?
- How honest do you think the content is?
- Can you define the word 'stereotype'?
- What does the source reveal about the dangers of stereotyping?
- Do any of the extracts imply anything about problems faced by immigrants?
- Why do you think people from the Caribbean wanted to come and work and settle in Britain?
- From your own knowledge, or can you find out, how were cities in Britain affected by the Second World War? What would life have been like at that time?
- How do you think people might have felt on arrival to Britain from the Caribbean?
- What other sources would help us find out more about Caribbean immigrants in Britain after the Second World War?

Exploring further

Students can now discuss and debate present-day issues of racism faced by immigrants and what can be done to overcome them.

Follow-up tasks
- Produce a leaflet on the lives of the pamphlet authors: Dudley Joseph Thompson and Hugh D. Carberry.
- Students could find out from classmates, family or neighbours if they have relatives or friends who came to Britain and, if so, where they came from and the reasons why they came. Present this information to the class.

LESSON 47

THE INDEPENDENCE OF GHANA

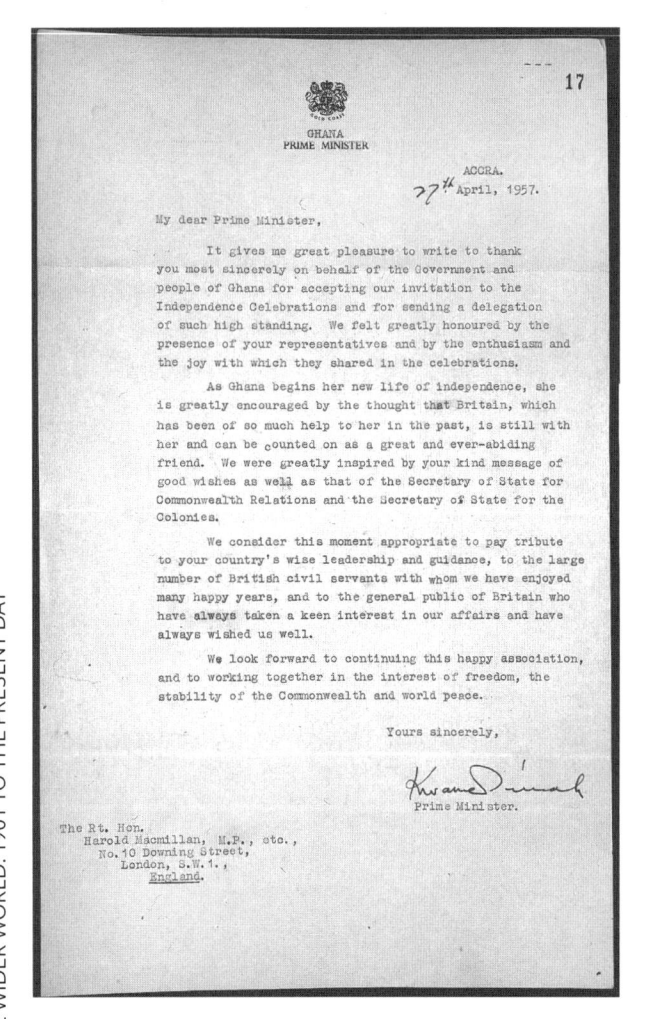

CONNECTION TO THE CURRICULUM

Challenges for Britain, Europe and the wider world: 1901 to the present day

Aim: To find out about Ghanaian Independence.

Historical figure: Kwame Nkrumah (1909–1972)

Sources: Letter from Kwame Nkrumah (PREM 11/1859); photograph of Kwame Nkrumah (INF 10/129)

TEACHER'S NOTES

What is this source?

The letter comes from records in the PREM 11 series, which covers the Conservative government in the UK from 1951 to 1964. It is about the representation of Queen Elizabeth II at Ghana's independence celebrations.

The photograph shows Kwame Nkrumah being carried from the Assembly after the announcement of the Independence of Ghana (previously known as Gold Coast) and is dated 6th March 1957. It comes from the Central Office of Information (INF 10).

What can we infer from these sources?

The letter is from Prime Minister Kwame Nkrumah of Ghana to Prime Minister Harold Macmillan of Britain. He is thanking him for Britain's acceptance of the invitation to Ghana's independence celebrations. We can infer that the people of Ghana are honoured that the delegation will be of 'such high standing', meaning Queen Elizabeth II will attend. The letter seems to be positive about the earlier colonial relationship between the two countries and the role of the British government and civil service. There is hope that this good relationship will continue, but importantly the letter also describes this change as marking a 'new life of independence'. The letter is formal, respectful and generous in its tone.

The photograph very much captures a moment in history. Kwame Nkrumah is being carried out of the government assembly. It is strikingly exuberant and informal. It reflects the sheer joy felt about Ghana's declaration of independence.

Why does The National Archives have these sources?

PREM 11 records are the Records of the Prime Minister's Office and are held at The National Archives. The office of the Prime Minister did not officially exist until December 1905 and the title was not mentioned in the text of any Act of Parliament until the Ministers of the Crown Act 1937. The photograph comes from a collection of 8,472 photographs compiled by the Central Office of Information and illustrate the geography and way of life in British colonial and Commonwealth territories. The photographs cover different topics including: agriculture, education, occupations, services and social conditions.

What is the context of these sources?

Kwame Nkrumah was the first Prime Minister and President of Ghana, previously known as Gold Coast, which became independent from Britain in 1957. He believed in Pan-Africanism, a global movement committed to uniting all Africans, beyond the continent itself, which originated from the resistance of African people against enslavement and colonisation. Kwame Nkrumah had been Prime Minister of Gold Coast since 1952 and continued in the role when Ghana was decolonised in 1957. In 1960 he was elected President with a new constitution. This meant that Ghana became a republic. It was no longer a constitutional monarchy with Queen Elizabeth II as Head of State.

💡 LESSON IDEAS

ENQUIRY QUESTION
What do these sources reveal about the British Empire by the 1950s?

Getting started

Use this source to extend knowledge gained in Lessons 18 and 28 on the British Empire and teach it alongside the lessons on the independence of Tanganyka, Barbados, Trinidad and Tobago.

In order to encourage your students to sharpen their historical skills for the interpretation of the letter source, introduce it using the 'mystery document' approach.

The 'mystery document' provides an exciting way to get students interested in a new history topic, encouraging them to make their own observations and to ask their own questions. Print out copies of the document or display a large version of the image on a whiteboard. Don't say anything about the document at this point. Tell the students they are first going to consider the source as an 'object' (how it appears and how it has been produced, and what these things can reveal), before going on to look at the contents. Give them just five to ten minutes to make their observations.

You could use the following approach:

- *Look* at the document as an object. *Don't read* it. What do you see?
- How was it produced? (Is it typed or handwritten? Note the crest and that it is numbered on the right corner.)
- How is the text set out on the page? (It's a letter, with the address at the bottom left, and it's been signed.)
- What does this reveal about the type of document this could be? (It's likely to be a formal, important letter between governments.)
- When was it written? (Look for a date.)
- Any other points to note?

Exploring further

Now encourage students to read the document and make inferences based on its contents. Here are some suggestions:

- Who has written this letter?
- Who are they writing to?
- What does the letter say?
- What is the voice and tone of the letter?
- How do you think this letter would be replied to?

Now introduce the students to the photograph. Discuss the value of using the photograph as evidence for the Independence of Ghana. What does the photograph tell you that the letter does not?

Finally, ask the students to write a short written response to the enquiry question: what do these sources reveal about the British Empire by the 1950s?

Follow-up tasks
- Find out more about Kwame Nkrumah and prepare a presentation on his life with a particular focus on the Independence of Ghana.
- Create a map to show the decolonisation of British territories in Africa in the 1950s and 1960s.
- Select one country and write a report on how they became independent.

LESSON 48

PAUL ROBESON

Empire News, 31st May, 1959.

Will Robeson sing in Trafalgar Square?

By PETER EARLE

THE "British Peace Committee," an organisation planning a great anti-H-bomb demonstration in Trafalgar Square next month, has announced that Paul Robeson will sing at the rally.

At Stratford-on-Avon, where Robeson is appearing in "Othello," his secretary said yesterday: "It is something Mr. Robeson might well do, or might not do. I do not know."

But he added: "But they should not give the impression that Mr. Robeson is in any way the instigator of the occasion."

One of the organisers of the huge rally—it has the indications of being bigger than the Aldermaston marches this year—had earlier said: "Mr. Robeson backed our campaign from the start. Now he has agreed to head the march and sing in Trafalgar Square."

CHAPLIN, TOO?

"We realise his position—he obviously does not want to upset the British authorities—but he practically insisted on playing a major part."

Robeson has been in England only a few months after years of trying to get his passport returned by the American Government who confiscated it on the grounds of the singer's political activities.

Many well-known Communists are connected with the Peace Committee, but a wide reaching body of people are also supporting or actually taking part in the demonstration.

They include Dame Sybil Thorndike and the Bishop of Llandaff in Wales. Leaflets which have been distributed in Yorkshire carry the names of Henry Moor, the sculptor, and John Braine, author of "Room at the Top."

I understand that letters asking for direct or indirect support have gone to other famous names in artistic spheres — including Charlie Chaplin in Geneva.

MINERS' SUPPORT

Scotland Yard has given permission for the rally—but I can reveal that more demonstrations at Rocket sites in East Anglia are planned; so are mass cycle rallies; and the release containing pacifist and anti-H-bomb propaganda of giant balloons in Central London itself.

One of the demands of the demonstration is for a Summit meeting. The rally is roughly the time when such an issue will become critical following the Foreign Ministers' conference at present going on in Geneva.

CONNECTION TO THE CURRICULUM

Challenges for Britain, Europe and the wider world: 1901 to the present day

Aim: To examine political protest in 1950s Britain.

Historical figure: Paul Robeson (1898–1976)

Source: Article from the *Empire News* (HO 382/6)

TEACHER'S NOTES

What is this source?

This source is taken from a Home Office file on Paul Robeson. It is an article from the *Empire News* on 31st May 1959. The *Empire News* was a Sunday newspaper that was eventually taken over by the *News of the World*, which went out of print in 2011.

What can we infer from this source?

We can infer from the source that Paul Robeson, the world-renowned singer, actor and civil rights campaigner, got his passport back in 1959 so that he could travel abroad. It had been withheld by the US government because he refused to disclose his political affiliations. We learn that he is now in Britain and appearing in the Royal Shakespeare's production of *Othello* and will sing at a peace rally against nuclear weapons in Trafalgar Square. The article hints at his left-wing sympathies and discloses the names of other supporters of the peace demonstration, including Charlie Chaplin.

Why does The National Archives have this source?

This newspaper clipping appears in a Home Office file about the American singer, actor and civil rights campaigner concerning the British government's approval for his visit to the UK. The file also contains other newspaper clippings, letters of complaint from the public and comments on his links to the communist party.

What is the context of this source?

Paul Robeson was a major talent. In his youth he was a sports star and he was also a bass baritone singer, actor and significant civil rights campaigner. He spoke out against segregation and discrimination in his country and was a supporter of trade union rights. In 1951 Robeson presented an anti-lynching petition to the UN. He was victimised in the McCarthy era, which saw a vicious campaign against supposed Communists in the US government and other organisations carried out under Senator Joseph McCarthy from 1950 to 1954. Many people, including Robeson, were blacklisted or lost their jobs. Robeson had his passport confiscated, which meant he could not travel abroad to earn a living performing. He challenged this ban in the courts for eight years.

Robeson was the first Black actor to perform the role of Othello, and the performance mentioned in the source, in April 1959, is the most famous.

The great 'anti-H bomb rally', referred to in the newspaper, took place on 28th June 1959, when 10,000 demonstrators marched to Trafalgar Square from Hyde Park for a rally against nuclear weapons. It was supported by trade unionists, peace organisations and left-wing political groups. Robeson spoke and sang at the rally.

Finally, the 'Aldermaston Marches', mentioned in the newspaper, began in April 1958. They were organised by the Campaign for Nuclear Disarmament (CND). Several thousand people marched from Trafalgar Square in London to the Atomic Weapons Research Establishment near Aldermaston in Berkshire. They wanted to show their opposition to the use and production of nuclear weapons. This became an annual event continuing into the late 1960s.

💡 LESSON IDEAS

ENQUIRY QUESTION
What evidence is there of anti-nuclear protest in 1950s Britain?

Getting started

Use this source to first of all introduce Paul Robeson; actor, singer and civil rights campaigner. Begin the lesson by telling the students about Robeson, using the teacher's notes. Robeson was hugely significant in the American fight for civil rights, which he saw as a global fight. His presence in Britain was important for Black communities in Britain. He was also the first Black man to play Othello on stage. He lived in London from 1927 to 1939, had performed free concerts for the Welsh Miners' Union and had likened the struggles of the working class to that of oppressed colonial peoples.

Introduce the source and explain that Robeson visited Britain in the summer of 1950 where he attended a huge anti-nuclear weapons demonstration in Trafalgar Square. The source is important because it provides a window into the anti-nuclear disarmament protests that took place in Britain in the 1950s.

Exploring further

Students become an 'expert' on the historical value of this source. You could use these questions to help support their interpretation of the source:

- What type of source is this?
- Why was a rally planned in Trafalgar Square?
- What were the Aldermaston marches?
- What support did the British Peace Committee have in the country?
- What were the aims of the demonstrators?
- Why had Robeson been unable to travel abroad before this visit to Britain?
- Where was he performing in Britain?
- What other sources would help us find out about anti-nuclear protests in 1950s Britain?

Follow-up tasks

- Write a chronology on the history of the Campaign for Nuclear Disarmament (CND) from its foundation to the present. Find out about the role of the CND today.
- Debate the issue for and against the use of nuclear weapons.
- Produce a leaflet on the significance of the career of Paul Robeson for the history of civil rights in the USA.
- Use the internet to listen to some of Robeson's performances of acting or singing; select one performance and write a review of it.

LESSON 49

LOUIS MARTIN

EVENING STANDARD

JAMAICAN MARTIN CARRIES FLAG
—OURS in HIS country

HAROLD PALMER: Kingston, Jamaica, Friday

Some remarkable decisions came to light here today. Guyana-born Clive Longe has been chosen for the BRITISH team in the European athletics championships in Budapest, and Jamaica-born weightlifter Louis Martin has been selected to carry ENGLAND'S flag at the opening ceremony of the Commonwealth Games here next Thursday.

By extraordinary coincidence, too, Scotland and Wales have selected weightlifters for the honour of carrying their flags. Chosen are Phil Caira, Scottish-born of Italian parentage, and Ieuan Wyn Owen from Caernarvon.

This is Martin's first return to Kingston, his birthplace, since he left home in 1956. His grey-haired and jolly father, who is a shipwright and over 70, has visited him in his camp billet.

"I am so happy," Martin senior told me. "I've waited four years for this, ever since Jamaica was chosen for the Games, but I did see Louis on television two years ago."

Bitter sweet

Martin, now 29, did weight training before leaving Jamaica and easily turned to weightlifting in England. And so on to glory and world championships. In the 1958 Commonwealth Games in Cardiff Martin lifted for Jamaica, but was disqualified for missing a lift. His wife, Ann, a Derby girl, arrives today to meet her in-laws for the first time.

"If I had stayed here I would never have made this top position in the sport," says Martin. "It may be a little bitter sweet for Jamaicans that I'm representing England, but it shows how much I owe to English coaching."

One who contributed in this way is Wally Holland, an Oxford optician and the weightlifting team manager here. He says: "I have never known anyone concentrate so much. It's like self hypnotism and he

Stranded Indians may miss opening

PORT OF SPAIN, Trinidad, Friday.—India's eight-man track and field squad for the Commonwealth Games are stranded here and may miss the opening of the Games in Kingston, Jamaica, next Thursday.

All airlines are booked up for Trinidad-Jamaica flights until next Friday, and the despondent Indians must go to the airport here every day hoping to obtain cancelled reservations.

does not know when the competition has ended."

Martin holds the world record lift of 420 pounds, all but an ounce or two. And he has a target of a 1100 pounds total in three lifts. He wants to be the first man under 20 stone to do this.

I gave Longe the news of his selection for Britain in the dining room at lunch-time yesterday. The Welsh party round him gave a cheer and called for celebrations.

CASH PROBLEM

The official notification awaited him in his room. It was a telegram from the British Board stating that the International Federation had accepted his qualification for the European championships.

Longe, now 27, came to Britain seven years ago. From serving in the Police band playing trombone and euphonium in Guyana, he joined the RAF. Kidded by Welsh international Hywill Williams to help form a decathlon team at their camp near Cardiff, Longe came fourth

in an RAF inter-station competition.

Now he is second only in the Empire to Roy Williams, New Zealand journalist and brother of Yvette Williams, 1952 Olympic champion and former long jump world record holder.

The biggest problem the athletes are facing here is how to spend their time because of the lack of facilities and money. They feel let down by the Government.

The £3500 proposed as expenses for the athletes of the home countries here has been turned down. So pocket money is restricted to 10s. a day for over 300 competitors.

However, Sandy Duncan, deputy team commandant, assures me, having cabled Commandant Earl Beatty, that extra money will be paid, as well as arrears, to the England team.

And Welsh team manager Ted Hopkins says: "I'm sure Wales will do something."

CONCESSION

Duncan did a good piece of negotiation, and not only for the England team, when he persuaded the organisers to allow the stadium here to be used by the jumpers for training. The other facilities were useless.

Dorothy Shirley says she has not been able to do any jumping for nearly three weeks. She is now relishing the chance of enjoying the good conditions in the stadium.

The three miles event will now be run as one final race on August 8, although there is an entry of 28 at present, the addition to the original 27 being Bill Baillie of New Zealand.

And Mary Rand and six others involved in two events which

LOUIS MARTIN
First visit since 1956.

were due to clash will now welcome the news that the start of the long jump is to be half-an-hour earlier. That means it will be taking place two hours before the 80 metres hurdles final on the last day, August 13.

● The British athletes here have sent a telegram to Alf Ramsey giving their best wishes to the England soccer team in the World Cup Final.

> **CONNECTION TO THE CURRICULUM**
> Challenges for Britain, Europe and the wider world: 1901 to the present day
> **Aim:** To find out about the weightlifter Louis Martin.
> **Historical figure:** Louis Martin (1936–2015)
> **Source:** Extract from the *Evening Standard* (DO 163/113)

TEACHER'S NOTES

What is this source?

This is an extract from the *Evening Standard* newspaper in 1966, published just over a week before the Commonwealth Games commenced in Kingston, Jamaica.

What can we infer from this source?

This document is a newspaper extract and we can read the headline and the introductory paragraph. We can also see that the author was a man called Harold Palmer, a sports journalist, and that he was writing from Kingston in Jamaica. To the right of the article, there is a photograph of a weightlifter who is Black.

The headline reads 'Jamaican Martin carries flag – OURS in HIS country'. Reading on, we understand that 'Martin' is Louis Martin, a Jamaican-born weightlifter, who has been chosen to carry England's flag at the opening ceremony of the Commonwealth Games.

Although the writer doesn't explicitly express disapproval in his description, we can infer that he considers this an unusual turn of events. The headline about 'our flag' being carried in 'his country' suggests that the author does not see Louis Martin as 'English'. In fact, the headline polarises Martin from the country in which he now lives, by describing Jamaica as 'his' country and the English flag as 'ours'. It also makes a division between Martin and the readership of the newspaper, 'us' and 'them', as though Martin doesn't belong.

Why does The National Archives have this source?

This document is held within a Dominions' Office file, which became known as the Commonwealth Relations Office in 1947. In 1966 the Commonwealth Relations Office and the Colonial Office merged to form a single Commonwealth Office, responsible for managing the relations with former colonial territories as they became independent members of the Commonwealth.

What is the context of this source?

The Commonwealth Games were originally known as the British Empire Games, the first of which was held in 1930. In 1954, the name was changed to the British Empire and Commonwealth Games, and in 1970 changed again, with the removal of the word 'Empire', to the British Commonwealth Games. In 1978 it became the Commonwealth Games.

Louis Martin was born in Kingston, Jamaica, in 1935 and came to Britain in the 1950s as part of the Windrush generation. He set up home in Derby and began to pursue an interest in weightlifting.

In the 1958 Commonwealth Games he represented Jamaica, but the following year he won a world title whilst competing for Britain. Further successes included a bronze medal representing Great Britain in Rome, 1960, and silver in Tokyo in 1964. He then took a third gold medal for Team England in 1970 in Edinburgh. Martin is often viewed as the most successful lifter of all time.

In 1964, Martin married a White woman from Derby, Ann Robinson. This was one of the first high-profile interracial marriages, and photographs of their wedding appeared in the *Sunday Times* supplement. In 1965, Martin was awarded an MBE by the Queen for services to weightlifting.

💡 LESSON IDEAS

ENQUIRY QUESTION
What does this document reveal about attitudes to race in 1960s Britain?

Getting started

Use this document to introduce students to Louis Martin and attitudes to race in 1960s Britain.

Ask the students to read the headline and introductory paragraph of the article. Use the following questions to prompt discussion:

- What is the author describing?
- How does he feel about events and why? How can you infer this from the text?
- Do the students think this would have been a widespread opinion of events at the time? Why? Why not?
- What does this document reveal about attitudes to race in 1960s Britain?

Exploring further

Use contemporary newspaper articles to investigate the lives of other Black athletes who have represented Team GB, for example, Harry Edward, Dame Kelly Holmes and Sir Mo Farah.

Follow-up tasks

- Listen to the audio interview of Louis Martin by Jan Rogers in 1998, which can be accessed at **https://sounds.bl.uk/Oral-history/Sport/021M-C0900X03039X-0100V0**.

LESSON 50

IMMIGRANT EXPERIENCES IN 1960s BRITAIN

4. The fact is that immigrants do face special problems in finding somewhere to live. They have seldom been able to arrange for any accommodation before they arrive and their first need is to get a roof over their heads; they frequently turn for help to compatriots who have preceded them to an unfamiliar land and who are usually anxious to help newcomers who have nowhere else to go. Both parties therefore frequently accept conditions which otherwise would be regarded as intolerable. Subsequently the immigrant finds it difficult to get anything better. Many immigrants are anxious to save as

high a proportion of their wages as possible and may be unwilling to pay more than the absolute minimum in rent, and it has to be remembered that many come from a climate where people are able and accustomed to spend more time out of doors and correspondingly less time in their houses than in this country. Some landlords are reluctant to let rooms to coloured people, and in addition, not having lived in this country before, immigrants have no previous period of residence which would help them to qualify for a local authority house. The fact that they often move from one part of the country to another may mean that in practice it is pointless for them to add their names to the housing waiting list of a particular authority.

6. We realise that there are no quick and easy solutions to the housing problem in the big cities. But present-day conditions are so bad that some immediate improvement is essential. We use the words " some improvement " quite deliberately, because we consider that action should be taken now, rather than it being deferred until perfect standards of housing are attainable. There is a real danger of a remote ideal being an enemy of an attainable good.

CONNECTION TO THE CURRICULUM

Challenges for Britain, Europe and the wider world: 1901 to the present day

Aim: To understand issues faced by Commonwealth immigrants in 1960s Britain.

Historical event: Immigrant experiences in 1960s Britain

Source: Extracts from the report by the Commonwealth Immigrant's Advisory Council (HLG 39/32)

Caution: This source contains language that is inappropriate and unacceptable today.

TEACHER'S NOTES

What is this source?
These are three short extracts from a report by the Commonwealth Immigrant's Advisory Council, July 1963.

What can we infer from this source?
The source gives some information on the experience of immigrants in Britain in terms of finding accommodation. It clearly highlights the discrimination experienced by many. We can infer that relations with the existing population are often hostile as many landlords are reluctant to rent to immigrants. It also points out the shortage of decent housing stock generally. It was difficult for immigrants to get on waiting lists for council housing without previous residency or if they were forced to move to find work and live in a new city. The source reveals nothing about the culture immigrants bring or the contribution they make in terms of public services and the economy.

Why does The National Archives have this source?
The extracts come from a report by the Commonwealth Immigrant's Advisory Council, July 1963. The report looked into housing for immigrants and is held by the Government's Ministry for Housing and Local Government.

What is the context of this source?
Not all Commonwealth immigrants were welcomed by White British communities. Despite the shortage of labour in the 1950s and 1960s, some still found it difficult to get decent jobs or accommodation. Often they were forced to accept jobs which they were over-qualified for, or they were paid less than White workers.

Most of the accommodation available was in poor inner city areas. Even if immigrants did have enough money to rent better-quality housing, many had to face the fact that some landlords refused to rent to Black people. They would be confronted with insulting signs in house windows that said, 'Rooms to let: no dogs, no coloureds'. By the early 1960s, an estimated 600,000 slums remained. Successive governments favoured high-rise tower blocks as the solution for slum clearance.

In 1958, in areas where larger numbers of West Indians lived, there were outbreaks of violent attacks against them. In particular, in Nottingham and in Notting Hill in London, mobs of White people attacked Black people in the streets and in their homes.

There were calls for greater controls on immigration, which resulted in the Commonwealth Immigrants Act of 1962. In the same year, the Home Secretary appointed a Commonwealth Immigrant's Advisory Council, which had a secretary from the Home Office and produced regular reports.

In 1965 the Race Relations Act was introduced to outlaw discrimination on the grounds of race. Yet more legislation, in the form of the Commonwealth Immigrants Act of 1968 and 1971, further restricted British citizenship.

Commonwealth immigrants had been invited to come to Britain. To be discriminated against was a shock that they had not been prepared for. Some returned to the Caribbean but many remained despite the difficulties they faced. They worked hard and contributed to British society. Today, later generations still face inequalities in terms of housing, the workplace and in the social services.

💡 LESSON IDEAS

ENQUIRY QUESTION
What does this source reveal about the experience of Commonwealth immigrants in Britain?

Getting started

Use this source to look at the experience of migrants in Britain during the 1960s. What were their relations with the existing population? What other difficulties did they face? How were they affected by changes in law concerning immigration and race relations?

Students discuss these questions in small groups and report back:

- What type of source is this?
- What problems do immigrants face when trying to find somewhere to live?
- How would these experiences make them feel?
- Why does the report say 'some improvement' in housing is necessary immediately?

Exploring further

Move on to consider what the source does not reveal.

- What other difficulties might immigrants experience when moving to Britain at this time?
- What contribution did immigrants make to society?

Select extracts to share with students from the film *You in Your Small Corner*, available for free from the British Film Institute. This drama, originally written for the stage by Jamaican-born dramatist Barry Reckord, is about a student confronting race and class divide in 1960s Brixton. Available at: **https://player.bfi.org.uk/free/film/watch-you-in-your-small-corner-1962-online**.

Follow-up tasks ✏️

- Teachers consult *Black and British: A Forgotten History* by David Olusoga for detail on this decade.

LESSON 51

THE INDEPENDENCE OF TANGANYIKA

> **CONNECTION TO THE CURRICULUM**
>
> Challenges for Britain, Europe and the wider world: 1901 to the present day
>
> **Aim:** To find out about the Independence of Tanganyika.
>
> **Historical event:** The Independence of Tanganyika (1961)
>
> **Source:** Photograph entitled 'Crowds campaign for Independence, March 1961' (CO 1069/166 (12))

TEACHER'S NOTES

What is this source?

A photograph entitled 'Crowds campaign for Independence, March 1961' from a file containing material concerning the constitutional conference relating to a visit by Iain Macleod, Secretary of State for the Colonies, to Tanganyika in 1961.

What can we infer from this source?

This is a crowd, predominately of women, demonstrating in favour of independence for Tanganyika. The caption says 'crowds campaign', so it is unlikely to be a photograph celebrating a declaration of independence. The photograph suggests that the women are standing by the side of the road, possibly waving at somebody, perhaps to get the attention of some official, maybe Iain Macleod, the visiting Secretary of State for the Colonies. The banner in the crowd calls for 'Freedom 1961'.

Why does The National Archives have this source?

This is a record from the government's Colonial Office and it concerns a visit of the Secretary of State for the Colonies to Tanganyika.

What is the context of this source?

Tanganyika formed part of the German colony of German East Africa before the First World War. However, during the East African Campaign of the First World War, it was occupied by the British and the Belgians. Britain held it as a League of Nations mandated territory when it was renamed as Tanganyika. From 1945, Britain held it as a United Nations trust territory. Tanganyika gained Independence from Britain on 9th December 1961. The country became a republic one year later. Julius Nyerere was the first Prime Minister of the independent Tanganyika and later became the first President of the new state of Tanzania (Tanganyika and Zanzibar) in April 1964. Nyerere was also central to the Organization of African Unity, now the African Union.

💡 LESSON IDEAS

ENQUIRY QUESTION
What does this source reveal about the British Empire by the 1960s?

Getting started

Use this source to extend the knowledge gained in Lessons 18 and 28 on the British Empire and link it with the lessons on the independence of Ghana, Barbados, Trinidad and Tobago.

In order to encourage your students to develop their observational skills for the interpretation of this source, introduce it using the 'five-second rule'. Do not supply them with the caption. Give the class just five seconds to look at the photograph on a whiteboard or printout. Ask them to remember anything they notice. Repeat a second time, but give them ten seconds to view it. What else they have noticed?

Exploring further

Now reveal the image for five to ten minutes and ask the students to jot down all the points they can make about the source. Then get the students to share their notes as you discuss the enquiry question: what does this source reveal about the British Empire by the 1960s?

Suggested prompt questions for discussion:

- Can you describe the scene?
- What is the possible message of the photograph?
- What are the people doing in the photograph?
- What does the image reveal which a written document might not?

Finally, give the class the original caption: 'Crowds campaign for Independence, March 1961'
- Does this now affect our understanding of the photograph?
- What other sources would help us to find out more about the Independence of Tanganyika?

Follow-up tasks

- Write a presentation on how Tanganyika achieved independence.
- Create a map to show the decolonisation of British territories in Africa in the 1950s and 1960s.
- Watch the short film *Tanganyika Independent 1961* from the Pathé film archive, showing independence celebrations in Tanganyika: **www.britishpathe.com/video/tanganyika-independent**

LESSON 52

THE INDEPENDENCE OF TRINIDAD AND TOBAGO

> PRINCESS ROYAL OPENS TRINIDAD AND TOBAGO PARLIAMENT.
>
> Princess Royal, who is representing the Queen at the Trinidad and Tobago independence celebrations, reads the Speech from the Throne during the State Opening of the Parliament of Trinidad and Tobago in the Legislative Council Chamber at the Red House.
>
> Seated on either side of Princess Royal are the Governor, Sir Solomon Hochoy, and Lady Hochoy.
>
> R.7953 (KT 16).
> September 1962.

CONNECTION TO THE CURRICULUM

Challenges for Britain, Europe and the wider world: 1901 to the present day

Aim: To find out about the Independence of Trinidad and Tobago.

Historical event: Independence of Trinidad and Tobago (1962)

Source: Photograph captioned 'Princess Royal opens Trinidad and Tobago Parliament' (INF 10/361 (4))

TEACHER'S NOTES

What is this source?

This photograph is held within the 'British Empire Collection of Photos' as part of the Central Office of Information files.

What can we infer from this source?

This is a black-and-white photograph, set within a very grand room. There are large windows and ornate columns, and a raised stage. Through one window, we can glimpse a flying flag. The room is full of people, many of them seated, dressed smartly in suits and listening intently, suggesting a formal event.

On the stage there is a beautifully dressed woman sitting on a decorated chair. She is possibly someone of great importance, and is reading aloud to those around her. There are two further seated figures, and men standing dressed in military uniform. In front of the stage are two men, possibly judges, suggesting that this event is legally important. Most of the seated men are Black, but the two men standing on the stage, along with the woman seated in the central chair, are White.

The caption reads that the Princess Royal is representing the Queen at the Trinidad and Tobago Independence celebrations; the photograph shows the State Opening of their parliament. With her are the Governor Sir Soloman Hochoy and his wife Lady Hochoy.

The photograph is dated September 1962, shortly after Trinidad and Tobago gained independence from Britain on 31st August. The Central Office of Information have compiled official photographs of this event, as they were responsible for the government's marketing and communications.

Why does The National Archives have this source?

This document is held within a Central Office of Information file relating to events in Trinidad and Tobago from 1955 to 1962.

What is the context of this source?

On the 31st August 1962, Trinidad and Tobago gained its independence from Great Britain. In the past, Trinidad had been inhabited by the Amerindians, before becoming a colony in the Spanish Empire during the 1600s, whilst Tobago had become a colony of numerous different powers until it was turned over to Britain (along with Trinidad) in 1802 as part of the Treaty of Amiens with France.

Following the abolition of slavery, Britain established a system of 'indentured labour' on the plantations. Chinese, Portuguese and Indian people were contracted under this system, with East Indians making up the largest numbers of indentured workers in Trinidad and Tobago. Indentured labour has been described by some historians as 'a new system of slavery'*. Trinidad and Tobago remained economically reliant on agriculture until the collapse of the sugarcane industry in the 1920s. As work opportunities and living conditions worsened, a labour movement grew and the 1930s saw an outbreak of labour riots. The Trinidad Workingmen's Association (TWA), and The British Empire Citizens' and Workers' Home Rule Party, both pushed for independence from Britain's colonial rule.

When Trinidad and Tobago eventually gained their independence from Britain in 1962, Queen Elizabeth II remained Head of State. In 1976, Trinidad and Tobago became a republic within the Commonwealth.

*see Hugh Tinker's book *A New System of Slavery* and Madhavi Khale's work *Fragments of Empire, Capital, Slavery, and Indian Indentured Labor in the British Caribbean*

💡 LESSON IDEAS

ENQUIRY QUESTION
What does this document reveal about events in Trinidad and Tobago in 1962?

Getting started

Use this document to introduce students to Trinidad and Tobago's push for independence from Britain.

Hide the photograph's caption and ask students to look at the photograph for two minutes.

Discuss the following questions:

- What can they see?
- What can they infer?
- Why are all of these people gathered and what do they think is happening?
- Why has the photograph been taken?

Exploring further

Now give the students time to read the caption at the bottom of the photograph. Has this changed their initial inferences about the image? What is their interpretation of the photograph and the event it captures now?

Follow-up tasks

- Ask students to research the lives of key figures in Trinidad and Tobago's push for independence, for example, Arthur Cipriani or Tubal Uriah Butler. Can they create a short podcast about their findings?
- Introduce students to the topic of indentured labour from India.

LESSON 53

THE INDEPENDENCE OF BARBADOS

BAR/LIN6 BARBADOS 196 SQCMS 300545G PRESS APPHO
LONDON 333 (AP) PM ERROL BARROW AND GOVENOR STOW
HAPPY AFTER LOWERING UNION JACK AND RAISING
BARBADOS FLAG AT MIDNIGHT CERMONY BRIDGETOWN. BOURD:

CONNECTION TO THE CURRICULUM
Challenges for Britain, Europe and the wider world: 1901 to the present day
Aim: To find out about the Independence of Barbados.
Historical event: The Independence of Barbados (1966)
Source: Photograph of Prime Minister Errol Barrow and Governor Stow (INF 10/48/17)

TEACHER'S NOTES

What is this source?

This photograph is held within the 'British Empire Collection of Photos' as part of the Central Office of Information files.

What can we infer from this source?

This is a black-and-white photograph and shows two men shaking hands. Both men are smartly dressed; the man on the right-hand side of the photograph is Black and wearing civilian clothes (a jacket embroidered with an emblem, a shirt and a bow tie), whilst the White man on the left is wearing some type of military uniform with medals.

The men look pleased and are smiling widely, both looking towards the camera. This suggests that the photograph has been captured for a specific purpose to show both men appearing united and happy. Behind them is a flagpole, which, along with the men's formal dress, suggests that there is some type of ceremony taking place.

Beneath the photograph is a typewritten caption, suggesting that it pre-dates the advent of the computer. The text tells us that the man on the right is 'PM Errol Barrow' (the Prime Minister), and the man on the left is 'Governor Stow'.

From the description, we now know the photograph shows the Prime Minister of Barbados and the Governor General celebrating the Independence of Barbados at the ceremony on 30th November 1966. The Central Office of Information compiled the official photographs of this event, as they were responsible for the UK government's marketing and communications at this time.

Why does The National Archives have this source?

This document is held within a Central Office of Information file relating to events in Barbados spanning 1943–1967.

What is the context of this source?

In 1625, an English ship, *The Olive Blossom*, set ashore in Barbados. Its crew declared possession of the island in the name of King James I and by 1627 the first settlers had arrived. The island was soon established as a plantation economy using enslaved people from Africa, which only stopped in 1834 with the abolishment of slavery.

By the late 1930s, poor economic conditions on the island had led to rioting. The Barbados Labour Party (BLP), which was set up in response to this unrest, pushed for social change. In 1955, Errol Barrow established the Democratic Labour Party (DLP); he was disillusioned by the BLP's lack of progress. Barrow and the DLP began the journey to independence for Barbados.

In 1966, Barbados became an independent sovereign state, with Barrow as the country's first Prime Minister. Sir John Stow, who had been the Governor of Barbados since 1959, was appointed Governor General on the date of independence. He was the chief representative of the Queen in Barbados, holding a ceremonial role.

Barrow made significant changes and improvements for Barbadians. He expanded the tourist industry, accelerated the process of industrial development, established free secondary education for all and introduced national health insurance and social security.

💡 LESSON IDEAS

ENQUIRY QUESTION
What does this document reveal about the Independence of Barbados in 1966?

Getting started

Use this document to introduce students to Barbados and the push for independence.

Hide the photograph's caption; ask students to look at the photograph for two minutes and write down everything they can see. Then ask the following questions:

- Who do you think the men in the photograph are? Why?
- Do these men look comfortable in each other's company? How can you tell?
- What are the men doing and why has the photograph been taken?

Exploring further

Now give the students time to read the caption at the bottom of the photograph. Does this change their initial inferences about the image? What is their interpretation of the photograph and the event it captures now?

Tell the students more about the Independence of Barbados, and in particular the role of Errol Barrow.

Introduce students to selected extracts from Errol Barrow's speech of 1986, entitled 'What kind of mirror image do you have of yourself?'. Discuss the following questions:

- What was he trying to achieve with this message?
- Why do you think Barbadians were inspired by this speech?

The speech can be downloaded in full in the resources section of the following webpage: www.caribbeanelections.com/knowledge/biography/bios/barrow_errol.asp.

Follow-up tasks

- Research further the lives of Grantley Adams and Errol Barrow and their respective parties, the BLP and DLP. Can you design a campaign slogan for each of their parties?

LESSON 54

SISLIN FAY ALLEN

CONNECTION TO THE CURRICULUM
Challenges for Britain, Europe and the wider world 1901 to the present day
Aim: To find out about multicultural Britain in the 1960s.
Historical figure: Sislin Fay Allen (1938–2021)
Source: Keystone-France/Gamma-Rapho via Getty Images

TEACHER'S NOTES

What is this source?

This is a photograph which shows Jamaican-born Sislin Fay Allen, the first Black woman to join London's Metropolitan Police Force, dated 15th February 1968. It is part of a series of photographs showing Sislin Fay Allen in training. The photograph was taken by a photographer for Keystone Press, a Fleet Street press agency. Keystone Press was later acquired by The Hulton-Deutsch Collection, now a part of Getty Images.

What can we infer from this source?

This is a publicity photograph taken by a press agency. The photograph clearly looks posed. Allen is shown attending at a staged motorcycle accident while six White constables and one White female constable observe. We can infer that it shows a significant turning point in police recruitment in terms of Black women. It also suggests that the police force was still a male-dominated environment with only one female observer present. Press agencies took photographs and sold them to newspapers at home and abroad so we can infer from the existence of the photograph that the first Black policewoman was a big story.

What is the context of this source?

A file held by The National Archives for the Metropolitan Police shows that other media outlets requested permission to photograph Sislin Fay Allen. Pathé News wished to feature her in a newsreel to be shown in the cinema. Before television, millions around the globe came to cinemas for their weekly fix of news.

In the same archival file, there is a request from *The Times* asking to interview Allen about 'the real problems which will face her – as a woman, as a coloured woman and as a coloured policewoman, when she finishes her training'. In response to this letter however, the police public relations officer says that as Allen was still completing her training she did not have enough police experience for such an interview. The folder also contains some racist hate mail and other correspondence which welcomed her appointment, so it is important to view this in the context of race relations in 1960s Britain.

Sislin Fay Allen emigrated to Britain in 1962 where she qualified as a nurse and worked in the National Health Service. She later went on to work as a geriatric nurse. In 1968 she joined the police, becoming Britain's first Black female constable. She was working in London at a time when there was a lot of distrust between the police and the Black community. Despite the importance of immigrant workers for the growth of Britain's economy and public services, many faced racism and discrimination.

Allen was a police constable in South and South West London. She also worked for a time at Scotland Yard's Missing Persons Bureau. Allen returned to Jamaica in 1972 to work in the police force there, until she retired. In 2020 she received a lifetime achievement award from the National Black Police Association. She died in July 2021. Allen was a trailblazer, making it possible for future Black women to enter the police force.

💡 LESSON IDEAS

ENQUIRY QUESTION
What does this document reveal about the importance of Sislin Fay Allen in the history of multicultural Britain?

Getting started

Students take turns in pairs to ask and answer the following questions:

- What type of source is this?
- What evidence suggests that this photograph is posed?
- What does the photograph reveal about the significance of Sislin Fay Allen in history?
- What others sources could be used to find out more?

Exploring further

- Learn more about Sislin Fay Allen at a police training session: **www.britishpathe.com/video/jamaican-policewoman-joins-force/query/Sislin+Fay+Allen**
- Prepare a list of interview questions for Sislin Fay Allen for a reporter to ask her on completion of her training in the police.
- Write a profile of her life for a class exhibition called the 'Windrush generation'.

Follow-up tasks

- Find out about Norwell Roberts: Britain's first Black officer in modern history (1967).
- Find out about highest-ranking Black female police officer, Commander Alison Heydari.

LESSON 55

THE RACE RELATIONS ACT 1968

For all complaints please give FULL DETAILS here:

My girlfriend and myself miss Sue Kepka arranged to go to the Palais on the evening of September 15th where we had arranged to meet three friends. We arrived at the Palais at approximately ten o'clock, we were both dressed for such a place and I was wearing a collar and tie, a prerequisite for the establishment.

There were about five couples in the queue and we joined the end of the queue for the purpose of paying our entrance fee. As we approached the glass door through which the patrons were entering, a gentleman from inside stood in front of the entrance and stated that we were not permitted to enter. I politely enquired as to the reason why, and he once again repeated that we would not be permitted to enter the premises.

I then remained outside and paid for miss Kepka (who is my girlfriend, she is white) to go inside so that she could contact our friends who were all already inside. Miss Kepka asked to speak to the manager and was informed that he would be available in approx 10 mins time. She then proceeded inside where she found our friends and explained the situation to them and also mr. Trevor, another friend who sings at the Palais. All these persons then proceeded to the entrance.

Signature of person completing this form: H. Horsford
Date: 2.10.73

Unless advised otherwise, please send this form to:
RACE RELATIONS BOARD
5 LOWER BELGRAVE STREET, LONDON, SW1W 0NR

CONNECTION TO THE CURRICULUM
Challenges for Britain, Europe and the wider world 1901 to the present day
Aim: To find out about the Race Relations Act of 1968.
Historical event: Race Relations Act 1968
Source: Complaint from Mr Lorne Horsford (CK 2/367)

TEACHER'S NOTES

What is this source?

This is an extract of a complaint made by a Mr Lorne Horsford, lodged against the Mecca Palais dance hall in Leicester, under the Race Relations Act of 1968.

What can we infer from this source?

This document has been handwritten in blue ink, possibly a ballpoint pen (popular from the late 1950s onwards), in quite a formal way. This, alongside the neat handwriting, suggests that the writer knows it will be read by other people, and that the words will be judged or assessed in some way.

The writer is describing his account of a recent experience. He talks about 'we', so he was with someone else when this happened. References to 'patrons' and queuing to pay the 'entrance fee' suggest that the writer and his companion were attempting to buy tickets for some type of entertainment venue. So, where were the writer and his companion going and why is the writer recording his account in this document?

Why does The National Archives have this source?

This document is held within files relating to the Race Relations Act of 1968.

What is the context of this source?

Mr Horsford lodged the complaint under the Race Relations Act of 1968, against the Mecca Palais in Leicester, following an incident that occurred on 15th September 1973.

The 1968 Race Relations Act (intended to strengthen the first race relations act in Britain, passed in 1965) made it illegal to refuse housing, employment or public services to someone because of their race or ethnic background.

Mr Horsford was Black and had attended the Palais with his White girlfriend. He was smartly dressed and sober, but was refused entry to the dance hall. His girlfriend, Sue Kepka, was allowed to go inside. Mr Horsford viewed these events as racial discrimination, believing he had not been allowed to enter the Palais because he was Black.

Once Mr Horsford had lodged his complaint, it was heard by the West Midlands Conciliation Committee, which held a meeting with senior staff of the Palais. The managers claimed that the reason Mr Horsford had been denied entry was based on a fight that had occurred weeks earlier in the Palais between a group of White and Black men. It had been agreed that Mr Horsford bore a resemblance to one of the men involved in the fight; this was why he had been denied entry to the dance hall. The West Midlands Conciliation Committee wrote to Mr Horsford and said that they thought he was the victim of 'unlawful discrimination'. They then sought to agree a settlement between Mecca and Mr Horsford.

Mr Horsford rejected the initial settlement of £5 proposed by Mecca and asked for £20. Records reveal that he hoped Mecca would refuse to settle and would be forced to fight the case; he wanted the injustice of events to be recognised. A settlement was not agreed and the case was heard by the Race Relations Board who decided to take it to court. The judge found that Mecca had discriminated against Mr Horsford because of the colour of his skin and awarded him damages of £40.

💡 LESSON IDEAS

ENQUIRY QUESTION
What does this document reveal about the Race Relations Act of 1968 and attitudes towards race at this time?

Getting started

Use this document as context for the Race Relations Act of 1968.

Take a 'mystery document' approach. Don't tell students anything about the document before you reveal it to them. Give them five minutes to explore the document and then ask:

- How has it been produced?
- When might it have been created and why do you think this?
- What type of document is it?
- What is it about?

Exploring further

After five minutes, encourage the students to dig deeper into the text to explore the following:

- What does this document reveal about race relations in Britain in the early 1970s?
- What do Mr Horsford's actions reveal about his response to the way in which he had been treated?
- What other types of documents could students use to find out more about race relations at this time?

Follow-up tasks

- Read Sarah Castagnetti's blog 'Young, British and Black: Opposing race discrimination', on which this lesson is based: **https://blog.nationalarchives.gov.uk/young-british-black-case-race-discrimination-1970s-dance-halls**.
- Introduce students to the case of Stephen Lawrence through Verna Allette Wilkins' book *The Life of Stephen Lawrence*, and how the Macpherson report into this case led to the amendment of the 1976 Race Relations Act to include the police for the first time.

LESSON 56

NOTTING HILL CARNIVAL

> **CONNECTION TO THE CURRICULUM**
> Challenges for Britain, Europe and the wider world: 1901 to the present day
> **Aim:** To find out about race relations in London in the late 1970s.
> **Historical event:** Notting Hill Carnival in the late 1970s
> **Source:** Frank Barratt/Stringer/Getty Images

TEACHER'S NOTES

What is this source?

This is a photograph that shows a policeman joining in with the festivities at the Notting Hill Carnival. It was taken by a photographer called Frank Barratt and is held by Getty Images.

What can we infer from this source?

This is a black-and-white photograph and shows a crowded street scene. Victorian buildings can be seen in the background of the photo, whilst the foreground shows a large crowd of people, all in a celebratory mood. They are smiling and look relaxed; some of them have their arms linked whilst others are drinking and watching the crowd, suggesting that this is a joyful occasion. The crowd is predominantly made up of Black people, although some White people are also present.

The central image shows a uniformed White police officer, standing with a number of black ladies dressed in carnival costume. The police officer has linked arms with two of the women and they appear to be dancing, which suggests that there is music playing and a party-type atmosphere. The police officer's hat and the style of the clothing of those standing in the street indicate that this photograph was taken in the late 1970s. The police officer and the women dressed in carnival costume appear happy and are smiling, whilst other joyful onlookers watch on.

The overall impression conveyed by the photograph is one of harmony and celebration.

What is the context of this source?

Documents held within Metropolitan Police files at The National Archives, contain many photographs of the Notting Hill Carnival from the 1960s and 1970s. These files are often entitled 'Photographs, Community Relations', giving us an indication that the carnival was something the police were interested in monitoring and recording; whether it was the relations between the Black and White communities in the area, or the police and these communities, is not clear.

Professional photographers, activists and carnival goers would have also taken photographs of this annual event.

Late 1950s Britain had a growing number of towns and cities that were racially diverse. Post-war economic migration, along with the numbers of Black people who already lived in Britain, meant that places like London were becoming increasingly multicultural. Yet this multiculturalism was also accompanied by racial tension.

In response to this strained atmosphere, Trinidadian human rights activist Claudia Jones organised an indoor Caribbean carnival in Notting Hill on 30th January 1959. Politically energised by the race riots of the year before, Jones wanted to hold an event that brought people together and celebrated West Indian culture. At the same time, political movements, such as the Coloured Peoples Progressive Association and the Association of Advancement of Coloured People, were also established.

The carnival ran every year until 1964 when Claudia Jones died. In 1966, the first outdoor Notting Hill Carnival was held. Today the Notting Hill Carnival takes place each year on the August bank holiday weekend.

💡 LESSON IDEAS

ENQUIRY QUESTION

What does this document reveal about the Notting Hill Carnival in the late 1970s?

Getting started

Use this document as part of your work to introduce students to post-war Britain and race relations in the 1950s, 1960s and 1970s. Ask the students to look carefully at the photograph.

- What can they see?
- When do they think it was taken?
- What event or gathering is it showing?
- Why do they think it was taken?
- What does it reveal about race relations in London at this time?

Exploring further

You can now move on from the source to a more general exploration of the Notting Hill Carnival.

- Why do students think the Notting Hill Carnival was established by Claudia Jones?
- What had been happening across Britain at this time and how would this have influenced her decision to organise the event?

Choose some visual sources from the online exhibition produced by the Black Cultural Archives about the Notting Hill Carnival to support this part of the lesson, available at: **https://artsandculture.google.com/exhibit/a-history-of-notting-hill-carnival-black-cultural-archives/eALiDoHj8Po6Kg**.

For example, you could split the class into groups, give each group one of the photographs and ask them to analyse what more it can tell us about the Notting Hill Carnival.

The sources and the students' analysis of them can be brought together into a class presentation or display on the Notting Hill Carnival.

Follow-up tasks

- Introduce students to Fiona Compton's interview about the origins of the Notting Hill Carnival at: **www.shadepodcast.co.uk**.
- Introduce students to extracts of Isaac James's essay 'Welcome to the Masquerade: How Carnival Makes Space for Everyone' from the book *Black Joy*, edited by Charlie Brinkhurst-Cuff and Timi Sotire.
- Explore the Black Cultural Archives online exhibitions at: **www.bcaexhibits.org**.
- In further lessons, students could investigate some of the racial tensions that existed in the late 1950s by studying the race riots in Nottingham or Notting Hill, or the death of Kelso Cochrane and the influence of Oswald Mosley's movement on the youths involved.

LESSON 57

THE BRITISH BLACK PANTHERS

CONNECTION TO THE CURRICULUM
Challenges for Britain, Europe and the wider world: 1901 to the present day
Aim: To find out about Black Power in 1970s Britain.
Historical group: British Black Panthers (1968–1973)
Source: 'Solidarity with Anguilla Protest', Express/Stringer/Getty Images

📖 TEACHER'S NOTES

What is this source?

This is a photograph (held by Getty images) showing a protest supported by the Black Panther Movement, in solidarity with Anguilla against the British invasion of the island. The protestors have been photographed at Piccadilly Circus, London, on 24th March 1969. The Black Panthers were the largest Black Power organisation in Britain at this time.

What can we infer from this source?

This document shows a large group of people gathered together in Piccadilly Square, London, holding banners and flags. One of the banners reads 'Black Panther Movement' and another banner spells out the message 'Solidarity with Anguilla'. We can immediately see that this group has been influenced by the Black Panther movement in the United States and are part of the British Black Panthers; along with the banner, there is a large flag representing the image of a black panther. The crowd is calm, ordered and well organised and all of the protestors are Black. They are protesting against the recent invasion of Anguilla, by a force of British paratroopers and police officers under the instructions of Prime Minister Harold Wilson and his government. The British Black Panthers movement aimed to unite Black people across the country and to fight for their rights, showing their determination to actively resist and fight against discrimination.

To the right of the photograph, spectators are separated from protestors by a metal fence. They are a group of both Black and White people; some of whom might have been present to offer support and others who were possibly just travelling through that area of London when the protestors arrived.

What is the context of this source?

Documents held at The National Archives also contain files relating to Black Power demonstrations in the late 1960s and early 1970s. These files include copies of newsletters published by the British Black Panther Party, and original statements and newspaper cuttings relating to evidence against the Mangrove Nine. Inspired by the Black Panther movement in the United States, the BBP initially fought against police brutality under the leadership of Obi Egbuna. Egbuna was arrested by the police, arguably in an attempt to destroy the new party, and imprisoned.

Leadership of the BBP fell to Althea Jones, and took a change in direction. It began to organise local Black communities across Britain around the issues of racial discrimination and the impact on employment, poor access to education, housing, and legal and medical assistance.

The BBP became a well-organised movement that worked within communities and advocated working-class solidarity, along with the fight again racial discrimination. In 1971, the BBP organised a march of over 10,000 people protesting against the latest Immigration Bill that reduced black immigration. They also created a Youth League and defended the Mangrove restaurant by organising a demonstration against the police. They supported the Mangrove Nine who were subsequently arrested and sent to trial on charges of 'inciting a riot'.

💡 LESSON IDEAS

ENQUIRY QUESTION
What does this document reveal about Black Power in 1970s Britain?

Getting started

Use this document to introduce students to the British Black Panthers and Black Power in Britain during the 1970s.

Ask the students to look at the photograph for five seconds. What did they notice? What do they think is happening? Now give the students longer to look at the image. What did they miss previously? What does this photograph reveal about Black Power at this time in Britain?

Now encourage the students to spend more time looking at the photograph. Does this help us to define 'Black Power'?

You can also explore with students the Black Power Movement globally. Does this photograph reveal anything about Black Power in a global context?

Exploring further

Once the students have got to grips with this source, you can introduce them to examples of posters and art of the Black Power movement through the rich collection of materials held by the Black Cultural Archives. There are sources available at: **https://artsandculture.google.com/story/owVxDSDJDD4gIA**.

What more can these sources tell us about Black Power?

Follow-up tasks
- Teachers can introduce students to the source on Mangrove Nine, and the British Black Panther movement's involvement in events and subsequent trial.
- Choose an individual from the BBP to research in more detail. What else can you find out about their life? What do you think inspired them and informed their fight against racial discrimination?

LESSON 58

THE MANGROVE NINE

> Aug. 9th
> Demonstration / Political Statement
>
> We, the Black People of London have called this demonstration in protest against constant police harrassment which is being carried out against us, and which is condoned by the legal system.
>
> In particular, we are calling for an end to the persecution of the Mangrove Restaurant of 8 All Saints Road, W.11., a Restuarant that serves the Black Community.
>
> These deliberate raids, harrassments and provocations have been reported to the Home Office on many occasions. So too has the mounting list of grievances such as raids on West Indian parties, Wedding Receptions, and other places where Black People lawfully gather.
>
> We feel this protest is necessary as all other methods have failed to bring about any change in the manner the police have chosen to deal with Black People.
>
> We shall continue to protest until Black People are treated with justice by the Police and the Law Courts.
>
> Action Group for the Defence of the Mangrove.
>
> Copies have been sent to :
> Home Office,
> Prime Minister,
> Leader of the Opposition,
> High Commissioners of Jamaica, Trinidad, Guyana and Barbados.
>
> To The Prime Minister, RT. Hon. Edward Heath, Downing Street. S.W.1.
>
> Issued by H. ANTHONY MOHIPP, Barrister-at-Law. c/o 8. All Saints Road, W.11.

CONNECTION TO THE CURRICULUM

Challenges for Britain, Europe and the wider world: 1901 to the present day

Aim: To find out about the events leading up to the case of the Mangrove Nine.

Historical event: Trial of the Mangrove Nine (1971)

Source: Action Group Statement for the defence of the Mangrove Restaurant (HO 325/143)

TEACHER'S NOTES

What is this source?

This is an Action Group Statement for the defence of the Mangrove Restaurant. It explains their reasons for the planned protest march on 9th August 1970.

What can we infer from this source?

This document is typed and has also been annotated by someone writing in blue pen. The stamp on the bottom right-hand corner of the document indicates that it was received by the Home Office on 12th August 1970. The document is entitled 'Demonstration/Political Statement', emphasising the importance of this protest and the motives driving the group.

The statement makes reference to the fact that the constant police harassment of the Black community, and the persecution of the Mangrove Restaurant, are 'condoned by the legal system'. This places the finger of blame squarely on the government and those in control of administering justice across the country.

Why does The National Archives have this source?

This Action Group statement for the defence of the Mangrove Restaurant is held in a Home Office file.

What is the context of this source?

This Action Group statement was sent on 9th August 1970 to the Prime Minister Edward Heath. This was also the date of the Black Power Demonstration march that it presents the case for. The Mangrove Restaurant was opened in 1968 by Frank Crichlow and became a popular meeting place for the Black community. During the period of January 1969 to July 1970 it was raided twelve times by the police, who claimed that drugs were being used on the premises. No presence of narcotics was ever found.

In response, The Action Committee for the Defence of the Mangrove was formed. It included amongst its members Black barrister Anthony Mohipp. Mohipp was also secretary to the Black Improvement Organisation and he has handwritten the annotations on the Action Group Statement.

On 9th August 1970, 150 people marched to the local police station in protest against this racial discrimination. Violence erupted between the police and protestors. A plain clothes police officer was on the scene to take photographs that could be used to suggest that key allies of the British Black Power movement were involved in orchestrating a riot.

Nine men and women were subsequently put on trial at the Old Bailey. They were: Darcus Howe, Frank Crichlow, Rhodan Gordan, Althea Jones-Lacointe, Barbara Beese, Godfrey Miller, Rupert Glasgow Boyce, Anthony Carlisle Innis and Rothwell Kentish. They became known as 'The Mangrove Nine'. Although invoking Magna Carta and demanding an all-Black jury so that they could be judged by their peers, their requests were not met. However, Jones-Lecointe and Howe decided to represent themselves. After a trial lasting 55 days, all nine were acquitted of the most serious charges. This was seen as a success for Black protest and a judicial acknowledgement of racial prejudice at play within the Metropolitan Police Force.

💡 LESSON IDEAS

ENQUIRY QUESTION
What does this document reveal about the events leading up to the case of the Mangrove Nine?

Getting started
Use this document to introduce students to the case of the Mangrove Nine.

Ask the students to *look* at the document as an object. *Don't read* it. What do they notice about the way it has been produced and set out on the page? What can this tell us about the type of document it is?

Exploring further
Encourage the students to now spend time reading through the document.

- When was it written?
- Who has written it?
- What action are they proposing and why?
- What does this document reveal about Black Power in 1970s London?

Once you have taught the students more about the case of the Mangrove Nine and the context in which it took place, the students can choose an individual from the Mangrove Nine to research in more detail. What else can they find out about their life? What do they think inspired them and informed their fight against racial discrimination?

Follow-up tasks
- Introduce students to the work of Robin Bunce and Paul Field, *Renegade: The Life and Times of Darcus Howe.*

LESSON 59

SUS LAW

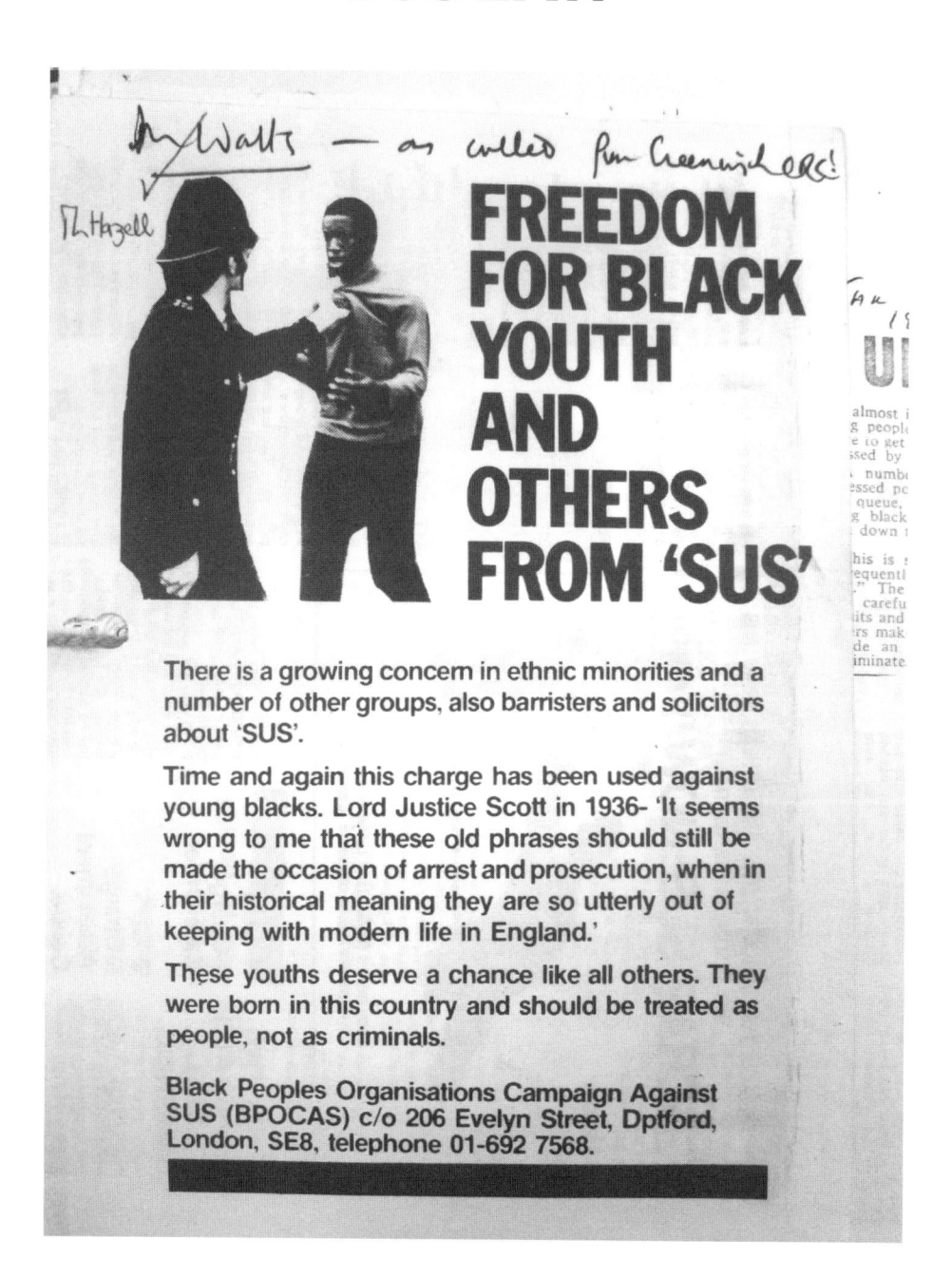

> **FREEDOM FOR BLACK YOUTH AND OTHERS FROM 'SUS'**
>
> There is a growing concern in ethnic minorities and a number of other groups, also barristers and solicitors about 'SUS'.
>
> Time and again this charge has been used against young blacks. Lord Justice Scott in 1936- 'It seems wrong to me that these old phrases should still be made the occasion of arrest and prosecution, when in their historical meaning they are so utterly out of keeping with modern life in England.'
>
> These youths deserve a chance like all others. They were born in this country and should be treated as people, not as criminals.
>
> Black Peoples Organisations Campaign Against SUS (BPOCAS) c/o 206 Evelyn Street, Dptford, London, SE8, telephone 01-692 7568.

CONNECTION TO THE CURRICULUM

Challenges for Britain, Europe and the wider world: 1901 to the present day

Aim: To find out about the SUS Law in the 1970s.

Historical event: Abolition of the SUS Law

Source: Flyer from 'The Black People's Organisations Campaign Against SUS' (HO 376/206)

TEACHER'S NOTES

What is this source?
This document is a flyer produced by 'The Black People's Organisations Campaign Against SUS'.

What can we infer from this source?
This document shows an image of a White policeman in uniform aggressively holding the front of a Black man's jumper. The policeman's face isn't visible; he is turned towards the man and his right hand appears to be clenched by his side. He could possibly be holding a truncheon or baton. The man is dressed in civilian clothing, looking directly ahead at the policeman, with his arms outstretched in front of him and the palm of his left hand facing upwards in a gesture of appeal. His facial expression is surprised.

There is a heading in bold font. It reads 'Freedom for Black Youth and others from 'SUS''. We can infer that there is an injustice; the policeman (who *should* represent law and order) is the antagonist, whilst the man is being treated with disrespect and aggression. The flyer goes on to describe how there is widespread concern about SUS, not just within ethnic minority groups, but also within the legal profession. This lends further evidence to the argument that SUS is being deployed unfairly. The word 'freedom' in the heading also underlines the way in which this law is being used to curb some people's rights and civil liberties.

Why does The National Archives have this source?
This document is held within a Home Office file relating to police relations with the Black Community from 1977 to 1980. The Home Office is responsible for security, law and order, and immigration.

What is the context of this source?
The SUS Law (the power to act on suspicion) dates back to the 1834 Vagrancy Act when 'every suspected person...with intent to commit an arrestable offence...shall be deemed a rogue and a vagabond'. This meant that the police could stop and search anyone in a public space if they were acting 'suspiciously', and could even arrest them.

During the 1970s and 1980s, the SUS Law was used by the police to target certain groups of people, particularly those from Black and ethnic minority backgrounds. This caused widespread discontent and anger, leading to campaigns such as 'Scrap SUS' led by Mavis and Paul Boateng, and the West Indian Standing Conference. The controversial SUS Laws were also a significant factor in the race riots of the early 1980s.

The SUS Law was abolished in 1981, and in 1984 the introduction of Section 1 of the Police and Criminal Evidence Act (PACE) standardised the power of police to stop and search people for stolen or illegal articles. PACE stated that there needed to be an *objective* basis for police suspicion and that 'personal factors' such as skin colour were not sufficient grounds to carry out a stop and search.

In recent years, new legislation has increasingly given the police greater power. This in turn has raised the issue, once again, that certain groups can become the target of laws such as SUS.

📖 TEACHER'S NOTES

ENQUIRY QUESTION
What does this document reveal about the SUS Law and the campaigns to abolish it?

Getting started

Use this document to introduce students to the relationship between the Black community and the police in the early 1980s.

Begin by hiding the text, and asking students to look at the image.

- What can they see?
- Who are these people?
- What are the men doing and do they appear comfortable in each other's company? How can they tell?
- What is the message behind this image?

Exploring further

Now give the students time to read the accompanying heading and text. Has this changed their initial inferences about the image?

- What is the message of the image and text together?
- What does this reveal about police relations with the Black community in the 1980s?
- What parallels and similarities exist today? What has changed?

Students could now design their own posters for an anti-SUS campaign in the early 1980s.

Follow-up tasks

- Ask students to investigate one of the SUS campaigns such as 'Scrap SUS'. They can then produce a short written essay on the question: How far did campaigns like this contribute to the abolition of the SUS Law in 1981?
- Introduce students to the events of the race riots in the early 1980s, for example the Brixton Riots.

202 Diverse Histories © Clare Horrie and Rachel Hillman, 2022

LESSON 60

THE BRIXTON RIOTS

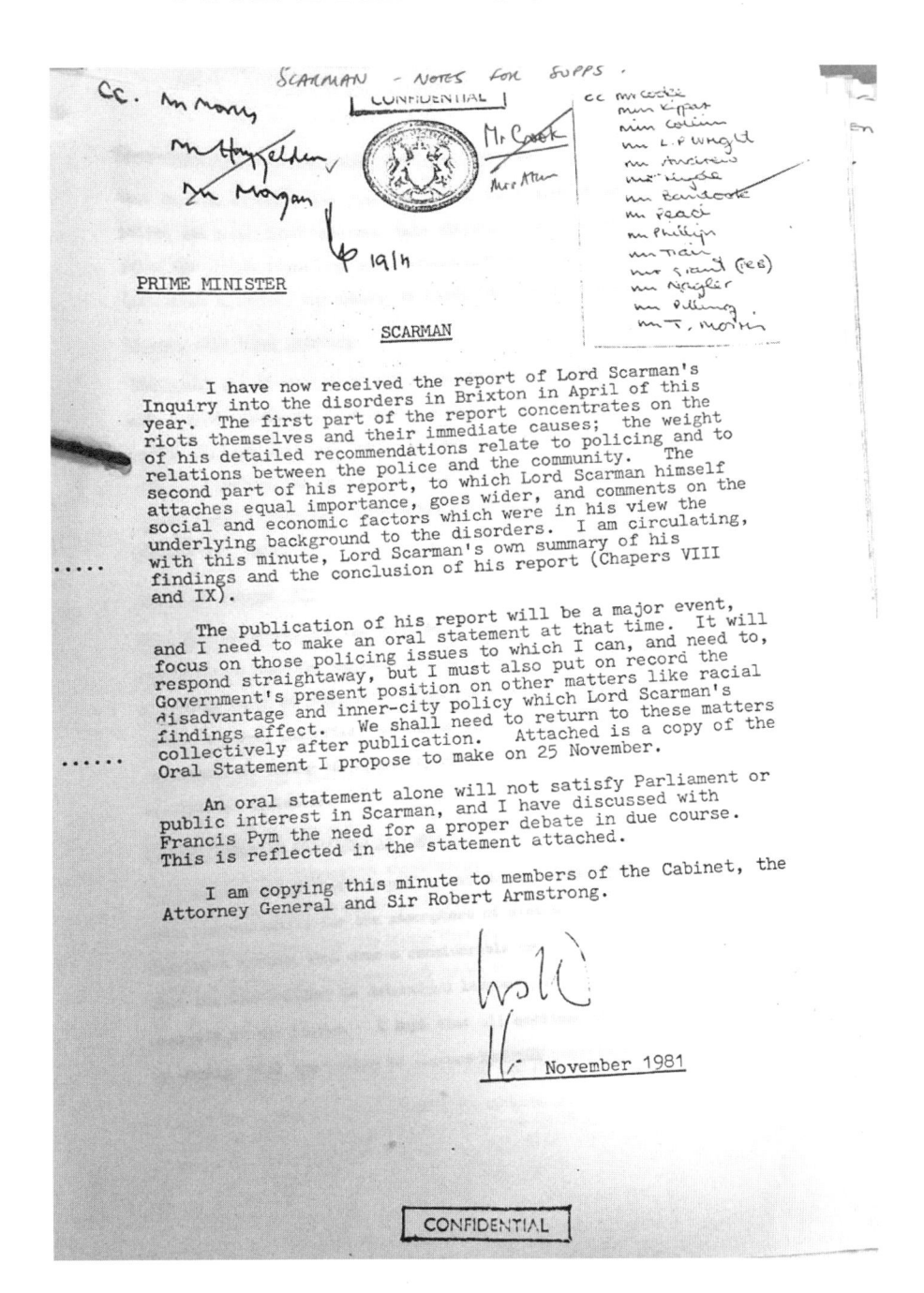

> SCARMAN - NOTES FOR SUPPS.
>
> CONFIDENTIAL
>
> PRIME MINISTER
>
> SCARMAN
>
> I have now received the report of Lord Scarman's Inquiry into the disorders in Brixton in April of this year. The first part of the report concentrates on the riots themselves and their immediate causes; the weight of his detailed recommendations relate to policing and to relations between the police and the community. The second part of his report, to which Lord Scarman himself attaches equal importance, goes wider, and comments on the social and economic factors which were in his view the underlying background to the disorders. I am circulating, with this minute, Lord Scarman's own summary of his findings and the conclusion of his report (Chapers VIII and IX).
>
> The publication of his report will be a major event, and I need to make an oral statement at that time. It will focus on those policing issues to which I can, and need to, respond straightaway, but I must also put on record the Government's present position on other matters like racial disadvantage and inner-city policy which Lord Scarman's findings affect. We shall need to return to these matters collectively after publication. Attached is a copy of the Oral Statement I propose to make on 25 November.
>
> An oral statement alone will not satisfy Parliament or public interest in Scarman, and I have discussed with Francis Pym the need for a proper debate in due course. This is reflected in the statement attached.
>
> I am copying this minute to members of the Cabinet, the Attorney General and Sir Robert Armstrong.
>
> November 1981
>
> CONFIDENTIAL

> **CONNECTION TO THE CURRICULUM**
>
> Challenges for Britain, Europe and the wider world: 1901 to the present day
> **Aim:** To explore the Brixton riots (1981) and how the government responded to them.
> **Historical figures:** Mrs Thatcher; Lord Scarman; William Whitelaw
> **Source:** Minute from William Whitelaw, the Home Secretary (HO 325/438)

Diverse Histories © Clare Horrie and Rachel Hillman, 2022   **203**

TEACHER'S NOTES

What is this source?

The letter comes from records in the Home Office. It is a minute sent to the Prime Minister, the Cabinet, the Attorney General and Cabinet Secretary. It is written by William Whitelaw, the Home Secretary.

What can we infer from this source?

It shows an urgent need to consider the findings of the Scarman report. The Home Secretary says that its publication will be 'a major event'. He suggests that there will need to be a debate in Parliament. The minute says that the report is critical of policing in Brixton and relations with the local community. It comments on the social and economic factors which contributed to the disorder. Whitelaw wants to explain the government's position on 'racial disadvantage and inner city policy' because these are affected by what is said in the report and it is implied to be part of public discussion.

Why does The National Archives have this source?

This is a government Home Office record. Home Office files reflect the diversity of domestic matters dealt with by the Home Office. For example, they can cover elections, fire services, Ireland and Northern Ireland, naturalisation, police, prisons or public order.

What is the context of this source?

Three days of rioting broke out in Brixton, London, in April 1981. The rioting was between predominately young Black men and the police. Over 300 people were injured, 82 arrested and 100 cars burnt. Damages were estimated at £7.5 million. These events related directly to policing methods, notably the SUS Law. The SUS Law allowed police officers to stop and search anyone if they suspected them of intending to commit a crime.

As part of 'Operation Swamp 81', over 1,000 people were stopped and searched in a week; most of them were young Black men. Added to this sense of discrimination, in an area of social deprivation, there was high unemployment, low wages and poor-quality housing.

The Scarman report, based on a five-month enquiry into events, was commissioned by the Conservative government led by Mrs Thatcher. The report concluded that there was no institutional racism in the Metropolitan Police force. This is different to the findings of the McPherson report in 1999 following the murder of Stephen Lawrence. Scarman's report said that closer links must be developed between the police and local services. He believed that 'Operation Swamp 81' was a serious error and that 'the police and community and its leaders both had some responsibility for the atmosphere of distress and mutual suspicion'. Scarman argued that racial disadvantage was a root cause. The recommendations in the report go 'to the heart of policing throughout the country'. As a consequence of the Scarman report, the SUS Law was revoked and a Police Complaints Authority set up, and later an Inner City Task Force.

In 1982, *The Voice* newspaper was founded. It is the only British national Afro-Caribbean weekly newspaper operating in the United Kingdom. In 1987, Black History Month was celebrated for the first time in Britain, the centenary of the birth of Marcus Garvey.

💡 LESSON IDEAS

ENQUIRY QUESTION
What does this source reveal about the government's responses to the Brixton Riots in 1981?

Getting started

Use the lesson as part of a study on community policing. By the 1980s, the relationship between the police and Black communities had seriously deteriorated. Police forces were accused of racism and using violence or intimidation to force confessions. The Scarman report highlighted that trust had broken down within these communities and police methods had to change. As a consequence, the police instituted more community-focused policing methods working with Community Support Officers. You could consider the following:
- How successful have these changes been?
- Are there similar challenges today?

Introduce this source using the 'mystery document' approach. Don't say anything about the document initially, but give the students five to ten minutes to make their observations. You could use this approach:
- *Look* at the document as an object. *Don't read* it. What do you see?
- How was it produced? (Is it typed or handwritten? Are there any crests or special stamps?)
- How is the text set out on the page? (It's a letter and it is initialled.)
- What does this reveal about the type of document it could be? (It's a formal, important letter between groups of people: the Cabinet, Attorney General and Prime Minister; there's a handwritten list of names at the top.)
- When was it written? Can you spot a date?

Exploring further

Now encourage students to read the document and make inferences based on its contents. Break the document down to make it more accessible. Define difficult language, including *Cabinet, Attorney General, Home Office,* and *Parliament*. You could discuss:
- Who has written this letter?
- Who are they writing to?
- Who is Lord Scarman?
- What does his report point out?
- Why is the publication of the report going to be a big event?
- Why does the writer think he will have to make a statement about the report?
- Why does he think that matters will have to be discussed and debated in Parliament?
- What is the voice and tone of this note?

Explain to students what the final report stated and discuss its impact. You can now link it to related legislation and reports from the 1960s to the 1990s. As a class, make a timeline explaining the significance of the:
- Commonwealth Immigrants Act 1962
- Race Relations Act 1965
- Immigration Act 1971
- Commission for Racial Equality 1976
- Scarman Report 1981
- Macpherson Report 1999.

Follow-up tasks
- Write a presentation on the causes and consequences of the Brixton uprising in 1981.
- Find out how events were reported in 1981 using newspapers and oral testimonies online.
- Visit the Black Cultural Archives at: **https://blackculturalarchives.org**.